VBS &OTHER SUMMER MINISTRIES

EVANGELICAL TRAINING ASSOCIATION
110 Bridge Street • Box 327
Wheaton, Illinois 60189

7 6 5 4 3 2 1
3 2 1 0 9 8 7 6 5 4

ISBN: 0-910566-57-7

CONTENTS

INTRODUCTION

Where is God during the summer months? The same place He is the other nine months of the year—omnipresent; wherever *you* are. Often churches become so engulfed in the maintenance of *programs* through the academic year, they lose sight of the relationship building purpose of ministry. The summer months come and everyone breathes a sigh of exhaustion, packs up for a program hiatus, only to return in the fall to an extended period of frustration as "church life" tries to revive itself.

Certainly devoted workers need a rest. They are, after all, human and subject to burnout. However, the needs of people all around us do not cease to exist. If anything, needs increase as the ills of society takes its toll.

An article in the Summer 1993 issue of *Leadership*, a journal published by Christianity Today, Inc., was titled "Rekindling Vision in an Established Church" and asked the question "Can old congregations dream dreams?" The article is a reprint from a decade before, published precisely because of the urgent quality of its message. The author, Dennis Sawyer, confirmed to the editors that the years had *enhanced* rather than diminished the truth of his message. Sawyer states, "Building relationships is more important than vision. It's through relationships that you inspire and encourage. Without relationships nothing happens."

Is nothing happening at your church in the summer? Evangelical Training Association has revived this old classic text (formerly titled *Vacation Bible School*) and added other summer ministry ideas. The ideas expressed are only a beginning. Many more exciting and inspirational doors to relationship building have been opened by people of vision who saw the idle summer months as a tremendous opportunity to affirm and win others for Christ.

DEDICATION

The Moody Bible Institute of Chicago, Illinois, was instrumental in the creation of Evangelical Training Association in 1930. For over sixty years, our relationship has continued to be one of mutual admiration and cooperation. One former faculty member, Doris A. Freese, Ph.D., Professor of Christian Education, was the author of our former *Vacation Bible School* textbook. Her many years of devotion to excellence in children's ministries has given inspiration to countless lay workers; many of whom only knew her from published works.

As Doris Freese is now with the Lord, we offer dedication of this revision to her, with profound thanksgiving and confidence that a continuation of relevant ministry would please our esteemed friend.

SUMMER MINISTRY OPPORTUNITIES

1

Vacation time is here! Even with family outings and community sponsored programs, children will too soon be asking, "What is there to do?" Adults can also succumb to a sense of adventure and break with the form to which they have been diligently loyal through long winter months. If the church provides meaningful answers, vacation time can be synonymous with excitement, spiritual impact, and growth for the entire family.

What an opportunity to reach our community with the claims of Christ through innovative Bible teaching and enthusiastic activities! Indeed, summer ministries can have both an educational and an evangelistic ministry to the local community. Its benefits are not limited to the young; the program can be expanded to provide spiritual enrichment for adults as well.

Most evangelical churches are still actively committed to utilizing the summer months for creative ministry. Some programs may take a sabbatical for three months, but active worship continues. Concentrated Bible study, creative expression of faith, and bolstering of family values are worthy goals often more satisfactorily achieved when the pressures of the academic year have eased.

The traditional Vacation Bible School has experienced a facelift, although the basic framework of Bible study, crafts, and recreation continues. Churches are finding more creative methods of implementing the program, thereby giving the appearance of a new structure.

Advantages of Summer Ministries

Utilize Leisure Time

Adding programs to the summer roster need not demand more from an already overtaxed volunteer pool. During the school year, students generally are activity-saturated. The vacation period, however, leaves free time for leaders and students alike to redistribute the workload. Summer ministry provides worthwhile outlets for time and energy. In some cases, working adults will want to schedule their time to be more involved with their children and the community. Most summer programs accommodate the season by being more casual in their approach.

Increase Teaching Impact

Sometimes *new* ministries are offered in prototype form during this season to give adequate time for evaluation. Concentrated attention to any one ministry opportunity is invaluable. For example, people who regularly attend weekly Sunday School receive 50-52 hours of Bible-oriented instruction *if* they maintain perfect attendance for an entire year. An additional 12-15 hours of teaching is received during a one-week daily Bible school; and twice that amount in a two-week school. For unchurched youth, the learning opportunities and loving concern experienced through this one opportunity are equivalent to half a year in the Sunday School program.

Translate a similar time equation to family camps and the impact on family structure is dramatically increased. Apply this theory to any special need your church may be experiencing and the summer months can soon be viewed as a productive and wise stewardship of our time.

Community Appeal

The informal, activity-oriented features of summer ministry appeal to all ages—even individuals who might hesitate to consider attending regular worship or Sunday School. Parents themselves are often drawn to a VBS program, either through an adult course, a parents' day, or a closing event.

Other ministries which are born from a common need in the community can soon take on a valuable life of their own.

➡ A summer project to roof an elderly person's home can grow into a significant support system, and outlet for ministry, to other senior citizens who are without families or adequate funds.

➡ Impoverished neighborhoods can become acquainted with caring people in an area church.

➡ Regions suddenly disaster-stricken might receive their emergency relief from a church otherwise regarded as just another large architectural structure.

➡ A community dependent on tourism can find a tremendous mission field coming to their door every year.

The opportunities for ministry are as varied as the community profiles.

Objectives of Summer Ministries

Reaching Others for Christ

"So faith *comes* from hearing, and hearing by the word of Christ"

(Rom. 10:17). Communicating the good news of Jesus Christ to others is an imperative of the Great Commission. Sharing God's Word and His love can be the first step in this process.

Bringing individuals to personal faith in Jesus Christ deserves prime consideration on the summer schedule. The believer who concentrates on understanding others better will begin to discern spiritual needs. Believers will be able to help those who are at a point of decision and guide them toward personal commitment to Jesus Christ.

Nurture Christian Living

Effective ministry results in more than mental acceptance of the Word of God. People must apply their Bible knowledge to Christian living. The witness of our life serves as an example to stimulate others to begin practicing what they have learned. Helping students apply Bible truths to daily experiences is an important contribution to the cause of Christ. It involves guiding others in making God's Word their standard as they seek to live for Christ. Even young children can learn to practice the teachings they receive. Everyone, at some level, can understand the needs of others, share in missionary experiences, take responsibility for cooperation in the church, learn consideration for those in the community, practice honesty, and apply self-discipline.

Values of Summer Ministries

Summer ministries effect more than the new people we seek to reach. Its value extends to the home, to church members involved, and to the community at large.

To the Home

We live in challenging days for families. The nurture and training of children by parents who love and obey God is central to the Christian home. Primary responsibility for the spiritual education of children rests with parents (Deut. 6:6,7; Eph. 6:4). However, church ministries, particularly those of the summer months, supplement the influence of home training through group experiences in worship, fellowship, study, and service.

Summer ministries reflect the church's interest in the entire family. It helps parents see the broader ministry of the church to their children. It helps individuals without a healthy family structure to find nurture from the Family of God. Everything from the simplest objects crafted to the intensity of shared experiences sends a powerful message from the church. Initial contacts can become bonded into meaningful, long-term relationships. Through the ministry of the Word of God and the Holy Spirit, homes can be salvaged, broken hearts mended, and families united in their love for Christ and each other.

To the Students

Summer ministries offer a multifaceted program to individuals of all cultural groups in a community. Bible study, expressional activities, fellowship opportunities, and recreation are planned to meet the spiritual, social, and physical needs of students.

To the Congregation

The combined efforts of church members in prayer, promotion, teaching, and publicity create a sense of unity and cooperation within the church family. Summer ministries help individuals feel the church is *their* church, the missionary program is *their* missionary program, opportunities are *their* opportunities. This often happens merely because everyone slows down long enough to observe them in a new way.

To the Pastor

Summer ministries provide the pastor with a different view of his church family, and perhaps his community. He can take advantage of the programs to observe the abilities and gifts of his people and to fellowship with them on an informal basis. Involvement in these programs by the pastor improves communication and understanding. Particularly with programs which incorporate entire families, the pastor can observe them as a family unit rather than the *age group* activity to which he may have associated the members heretofore. Contacts with parents and with community families (or lack thereof) enlarges the pastor's awareness of needs and can renew a vision for ministry.

To Christian Education

Summer ministries provide greater fulfillment of the overall goals of Christian education. Objectives and use of facilities are expanded. New people can become integrated into the year-round program and acquire appropriate balance and direction for their spiritual journeys.

The summer also provides a great opportunity for discovering and training new teachers. A wise leader can also learn from the strengths and weaknesses of summer programs.

To the Summer Ministry Staff

Leaders and followers alike have the unique experience of working together in a team relationship for a short period of time. Opportunities are built into summer programs for experimentation with new methods and new materials. The teacher's knowledge and abilities are expanded. The attentive teacher grows in understanding through more personalized involvement with others.

Leadership training courses can be offered to enrich experienced teachers and prepare new recruits. The training experience and confidence gained may encourage some to serve the Lord in other church-related ministries. Many young people, as well as adults, receive their initial preparation and experiences in Christian service during the summer months.

To the Community

While demonstrating the church's concern for people, these unique programs acquaint the community with the church's message and services. Racial prejudices and class distinctions are broken down when the church sincerely opens its doors to the community. Many families attend church for the first time through one of these special summer programs.

Summary

Summer ministries seek to combine Bible truth with creative experiences to promote evangelism and spiritual growth. Wise use of leisure time, increased teaching impact, thorough Christian education, and community appeal are sufficient reasons to launch a summer ministries program.

The values extend to the home, to the students, to the congregation, to the pastor, to church leadership and training staff, and to the community. Indeed, summertime can provide the church with a meaningful vacation outreach ministry!

For Further Discussion

1. Discuss the values of programs currently offered during the summer by your church.
2. Identify ways your community could benefit by a pointed program to a target group during the summer months.
3. What biblical imperatives justify an outreach ministry to the community?

For Application

1. Compare and contrast summer ministry programs now offered with programs during the remaining year.
2. What are the specific objectives of your current summer programs? How might they be enhanced through concentrated summer efforts?
3. Inquire about the summer programs of two churches in your community and compare the findings with your own church.

Organizations Which Can Help

In addition to contacting local agencies, the following ministries may be helpful to your needs:

The Bible League
16801 VanDam Rd.
South Holland, IL 60473

Christian Action Council
100 W. Broad St. Ste. 500
Falls Church, VA 22046
703-237-2100

Christian Council on Persons
  with Disabilities
PO Box 458
Lake Geneva, WI 53147
414-275-6131

Christian Military Fellowship
PO Box 1207
Englewood, CO 80150
303-761-1959
FAX 303-761-6226

Evangelism Explosion III Int'l Inc.
James Kennedy, Director
5554 N. Federal Hwy.
Ft. Lauderdale, FL 33307
305-491-6100

Focus On The Family
Colorado Springs, CO 80995
800-232-6459

MOPS International, Inc.
  (Mothers of Preschoolers)
4175 Harlan St. Ste. 105
Wheaton Ridge, CO 80033
303-420-6100

Prison Fellowship International
PO Box 17500
Washington, DC 20041-0500

Youth Challenge (drug rehab)
RD 2 Box 33
Sunbury, PA 17801
717-286-8007
FAX 717-286-8005

Willow Creek Association
PO Box 3188
Barrington, IL 60011-3188
708-765-0070
FAX 708-765-5046

VACATION BIBLE SCHOOL

2

For many years Bible-believing churches have sought to share their faith and knowledge of the Word through a concentrated week of study, crafts, and recreation known as Vacation Bible School or VBS. Although the concept is not new, and some have proclaimed it "dead," VBS remains a perennially *new* experience. Each year brings a new emphasis, new staff, new students, and hopefully, new spiritual growth.

History of VBS

The origin of VBS can be traced to the latter part of the last century. In 1894, a pastor's wife in Hopedale, Illinois, concerned over the Sunday School not offering a thorough knowledge of the Bible, conducted a month-long school with 37 children in four departments. In 1898, Everyday Bible School was held at Epiphany Baptist Church in New York City. Bible stories and Bible memorization were emphasized. In 1901, Dr. Robert Boville, executive secretary of the New York Baptist City Mission Society, held a series of schools. He is credited with formal organization of the VBS movement.

Response to VBS was favorable because worthwhile activities were provided for bored or idle children. The movement continued to expand. Here was an opportunity for Bible learning during the summer months when many churches were *closed*. College students and teachers, needed to staff VBS, followed the same vacation schedule as those to be reached and were therefore available.

VBS has grown from a limited venture into a significant church ministry. In 1923, the first VBS curriculum was released with kindergarten, primary, and junior materials for a five-week school. Today, VBS materials are a regular feature of many religious publishing houses.

The role of VBS in the total church ministry cannot be replaced by any other existing program. Consider the unique features of VBS. While VBS ministry begins with reaching students for Christ, it also seeks to send them out for Him. Once a student has accepted Jesus Christ as Lord and Savior, every effort should be made to draw him into the church family. Children, youth, and adults alike should share their newfound or renewed faith in Jesus Christ with others. An evidence of Christian growth can be seen in this desire to reach others for Him.

Basic Preparation

Initial Planning

Planning and preparation are key ingredients for a successful VBS. When carried out by dedicated personnel, who are guided by the Holy Spirit, the purpose of VBS will be fulfilled. Planning should begin several months in advance for best results. Clarification of objectives in the early stages of planning will influence the direction of all other decisions, especially staffing.

After objectives are determined, specifics such as type of school, curriculum materials, schedule, location, and finances will be more wisely executed.

Secure Approval

Regardless of who initiates the idea of conducting VBS, approval and endorsement should be secured from the church governing body which schedules church events and approves key leadership. This official group will be significantly instrumental in your program's success. The pastor may want to present the plan to the group himself, or he may invite a VBS enthusiast to do so. Offering a comprehensive picture of the VBS plan as a valid outreach ministry is essential for maximum cooperation and support.

Types of Schools

Organization and sponsorship of VBS may have varied features from church to church, but there are basic similarities. The objectives cited in the approval process should complement the type of school.

Single Church School

Most popular is the approach of a single congregation who is entirely responsible for leadership, choice of curriculum, staffing, organization, and finances of a VBS program. The church has sole control and can promote its own local church and missionary program. It can also direct the follow-up of VBS prospects for fuller church involvement.

Cooperative School

In a cooperative school, two or more churches share their resources, facilities, personnel, and materials to achieve together what they could not alone. Cooperative schools are interdenominational, denominational, or independent ventures. The larger supply of workers, better facilities, and combined finances provide some advantages. Greater public support from community organizations, as well as from a wider range of families, may result from this cooperative effort.

Limitations exist, however. Since in a cooperative school all churches share equal voice in planning, an evangelical church faces both risks and benefits when aligning with other community churches not of an evangelical persuasion. On the other hand, in a community where several churches of a common denomination or theological distinctive combine, the fears of compromised doctrine, unsatisfactory curriculum, and unacceptable staff are eliminated. Where problems cannot be satisfactorily resolved, a church should plan its own school.

Branch School

Similar to a branch Sunday School, a branch VBS is conducted by a church in a different location from its own building. Another section of the city, another community, a suburb, or a rural area where there is no VBS are suitable locations for branch schools. Workers trained, equipped, and financed by the local church assume responsibility for the school. Where possible, however, residents in the branch area are included in the staff.

Variations

Although VBS is usually held in a church building, there are numerous ways to vary the setting. Backyard or neighborhood schools may hold small classes in several homes. VBS could meet in a community or state park if permission is obtained in advance. A recreation or meeting room of a condominium or community center is a good location. VBS may meet in a vacant store, a tent, or vacancy at a shopping mall (ordinances permitting). The design of the school may break from traditional classroom appearance. With vision, creativity, and determination, meaningful ways to reach a community for Christ can be found.

Schedule

The planning committee is responsible for determining the dates, length, and hours of VBS. These times should be selected several months in advance and reserved on church and community calendars. Factors to consider include availability of staff, other summer activities such as retreats and camp, work schedules of adult and student assistants, vacation schedules, school and community activities, timing of VBS in other churches, and weather conditions.

Dates

VBS can be held during any portion of the summer season. Each time has its unique advantages and disadvantages to each community.

An early summer VBS begins immediately after the close of school. Children should still be in the habit of attending school and studying. It is likely the weather is milder at this time, making teaching and studying easier. On the other hand, children may be tired of the school atmosphere. Also, summer school and community programs, such as music and swimming lessons, may conflict with an early VBS.

Mid-summer offers opportunity to relax after school has closed and avoids conflicting with early summer school and community programs. The teaching staff and enrollment may be limited, though, since July and August are often popular months for family vacations.

A VBS program in late summer will fill the need of guided activities for restless children. However, holding training sessions for workers during the peak vacation time, prior to a late VBS, may limit staff participation.

Another possibility is to plan toward holding a modified VBS during other vacation times such as spring break or other school holidays.

Length

Some publishers offer both five- and ten-day programs. Others offer a five-day program with follow-up suggestions or alternatives to extended sessions. School objectives and availability of staff largely determine the length of VBS. The school must be long enough to be effective. Lasting Christian values can often be developed better by using a ten-day school. Some churches may want to try a one-day-a-week VBS for six or eight weeks. Others might find a need for one day at the beginning or end of the schedule devoted entirely to facility set up, registration, or special closing activity.

Likewise, the time of day should be thoroughly discussed. Cooler morning hours may be preferred by everyone involved. Children will have their afternoons free for outdoor activities. Unfortunately, few men are available to teach in a day-time VBS and more women are employed full-time outside the home which limits staff possibilities.

An evening VBS can possibly involve entire families. The program can be geared to family-units. Evenings, however, can be tiring for very young children.

Curriculum publishers of VBS materials usually offer balanced emphasis in their schedules. The materials are educationally sound with great emphasis toward hands-on learning. Most publishers include step-by-step plans for the overall program.

Finances

Churches that regularly hold VBS usually have a definite plan for financing the school. The planning committee must work within the VBS budget authorized by the church. Costs of curriculum, promotional materials, supplies, and incidentals are included in the overall budget. The choice of curriculum, craft projects, type of refreshments, or other extras will vary with the budget.

In cases where VBS is not included in the total church budget or the plan for financing VBS needs revision, alternative plans can, and should, be arranged. Explore other budgeted educational programs which might consider sponsoring part, or all, of the VBS program. A special offering day can be set aside for cash gifts or needed supplies. Individuals within the church who cannot participate in any other way may be willing to contribute toward "scholarships." Even a voluntary registration fee will help defer expenses, especially for a first-year ministry. In any case, the investment of a few dollars per person reached for Christ carries an excellent return.

Advance Planning

The planning committee needs to develop an operating schedule which includes every aspect of VBS. Checkpoints and dates for completing each stage of planning should be set. Publishers of curriculum frequently suggest a planning calendar in their materials which can be adapted to individual church needs.

Be sure to schedule training sessions for workers. It is an important part of planning. The preparation of teachers is a prerequisite for a successful school.

Summary

Broad areas of planning must be completed before personnel training, specific program planning, and preparation of materials can begin. Preliminary considerations include securing approval from the appropriate board of the church and appointing a VBS planning committee. This committee assumes responsibility for the details of the school including the type, schedule, finance, and promotion. It develops an overall plan of operation with coordinated daily schedules for each department.

For Further Discussion

1. Select a panel of three class members to discuss the best date, time of day, and length of VBS. The panel should be able to support their preferences when questioned by class members.
2. How can a diversity of activities be included in the daily schedule so that student needs and departmental goals are met?
3. In what ways can the results of a branch VBS be followed-up?

For Application

1. Make a chart of committees which are helpful in carrying out a small or large VBS.
2. Using a specific VBS curriculum, develop a planning schedule with suggested checkpoints until the school begins.
3. Prepare a sample budget of your next VBS program using an estimated number of participants.

Organizations Which Can Help

See also Chapter Three Curriculum Publishers.

Child Evangelism Fellowship
PO Box 348
Warrenton, MO 63383

Children's Bible Fellowship of New York, Inc.
 Division of Hope Town Resident Christian School
P.O. Box 670
Carmel, NY 10512

CHOOSING VBS CURRICULUM

3

Selecting curriculum for VBS is critical for it influences the entire program. Today, a variety of well-written published materials are available for all ages. Most VBS programs concentrate on preschool through sixth grade divisions. Materials are available from a few publishers for adults and teens. Before embarking on a curriculum search, consider the wide range of meaning which has been attached to the term *curriculum*.

Traditionally, curriculum referred only to a specific course of study. Teachers felt an imperative to adhere strictly to the printed material. Much to their frustration, they either could not fit in everything suggested by the publishers, or they wished to add some of their own teaching methods and could not.

At the other extreme, some adopt a more loose definition of the word; labeling all that happens to a person as curriculum. This generalization often does not provide enough structure. A framework is necessary for workers to understand the function of curriculum and to use it properly.

Many Christian educators would agree a balanced curriculum is a total program which, with the Holy Spirit's guidance, integrates lesson content with student experiences. Christ, the living Word, is presented both in content and experience.

The content of a curriculum should be faithful to, and firmly based on, biblical truth. In turn, Bible truth must be related to students in a manner which conveys understanding and integration into their experience.

Curriculum Components

Bible study, worship and evangelism, character building, Christian service, and fellowship give curriculum a sense of balance and completeness. If there is a lack in any of these areas, a teacher may want to emphasize some more than others. VBS curriculums are often centered around a specific theme which provides impetus for all activity and imagery.

Bible Study

"Be diligent to present yourself approved to God as a workman who does not need to be ashamed, handling accurately the word of truth" (2 Tim. 2:15). VBS curriculum should guide older students in learning to use their Bibles in study. Provide opportunities for students to discover the study passages for themselves. Be sensitive to the number of unchurched children you attract, providing Bibles and extra assistance. With younger children, Bible stories should be graded to the child's learning level and accurately presented.

Scripture memorization also can be a meaningful part of the curriculum. Key questions to ask when considering VBS curriculum are: How central is the written Word in the curriculum? How are students guided through the written Word to Jesus Christ, the Living Word?

Worship and Evangelism

Worship is a means of expressing adoration to God and of responding to biblical truths. Often a worship segment is scheduled after the Bible study session for the purpose of a genuine heart response to God and His truth. This is distinct from opening exercises when the group is rallied together.

Evangelism is central to the VBS program. Biblical truths must be presented in such a manner that unbelievers can hear and understand the plan of salvation. Bible stories and lessons should be examined for the extent and degree of instruction about salvation.

When considering the place of evangelism in the curriculum, ask: How are participants led to a decision for Christ? Is the gospel simply and clearly presented? Does the invitation allow for a natural, Spirit-prompted response? Are effective teacher helps provided for presenting and following up the salvation message?

Character Building

Curriculum should provide more than information about Bible facts and truths. The curriculum should aim for specific behavior changes, both in believers and unbelievers. Unbelievers can be encouraged to make a personal commitment to Jesus Christ. Believers need to be challenged toward Christian maturity. Activities and experiences which support and surround Bible truths are most effective in accomplishing these goals.

At VBS, students should be encouraged to practice genuine Christian living in their homes and neighborhoods. Demonstration of the fruit of the Spirit—love, joy, peace, longsuffering, gentleness, goodness, faith, meekness, and temperance—by the teaching staff will influence the students' personal Christ-like development.

Christian Service

Printed materials often suggest projects which contribute service to a church, community, or mission emphasis. An activity may be a one-day project or last the entire time of the school. Many churches fulfill individual interest and needs by developing their own projects. Care should be exercised in planning these projects to insure correlation with the curriculum content. If a project reflects the Bible lesson or its theme and is a natural response to the teaching, it will become more meaningful to the students. Projects which require personal involvement of the student are more satisfying than fund raising alone.

Fellowship
A sense of belonging and fellowship is essential to VBS. The amount of time spent in VBS allows many opportunities for interaction. Consider whether the curriculum encourages the proper measure of group and individual activity. A brief period for simple refreshments is usually suggested to reinforce much needed social skills. When a friendly, cooperative spirit prevails, the sense of belonging to the larger family of God increases. What potential VBS offers for not only making new friends, but Christian friends!

Standards for Evaluating Methods
Including both content and experiences in curriculum provides opportunity for a variety of teaching methods. Quality curriculum is complete, correlated, creative, child- and life-related, current, captivating, and conclusive. It should be evaluated open-mindedly for the flexibility it can bring to new and creative learning experiences.

Complete
Printed materials should provide sufficient illustrations, teaching aids, and suggested source materials to stimulate the experienced teacher while helping the new teacher. Unfamiliar methods should be thoroughly explained so teachers feel confident enough to attempt them.

Correlated
Coordination of ideas and activities increases the effectiveness of education. Since VBS tries to accomplish so much within a brief time, correlation is particularly important. Examine the degree to which departmental experiences are unified around meaningful themes each day. It is not necessary to have a uniform, school-wide, daily theme. Each department or grade may have its own. Bible stories, activities, workbooks, worship songs, memory work, crafts, and recreation should reinforce each other.

Creative
During the school year, students are exposed to a variety of teaching techniques and learning situations. It is even more essential, then, that creativity be used to stimulate learning during

vacation times. Look for curriculum which gives helpful hints for increased teaching flexibility. Also, student involvement and creative expression should always be encouraged.

In recent years, VBS publishers have produced wonderfully inventive study themes. However, cautiously explore a curriculum's spiritual content and purpose. These should never be sacrificed to creativity. A delicate balance must be attentively addressed by the curriculum selection committee.

Child- and Life-related

VBS materials must relate to the experiences, needs, and interests of the students involved. Guiding children to discover answers to life's problems from God's Word is one of the central objectives of VBS. To present Christ as the answer to life's problems, curriculum must correspond to the students' level of comprehension. The publisher's understanding of students is reflected in the choice of Bible lessons and supporting activities.

Current

It is natural for school-age children to compare VBS with other school materials. Most school texts and workbooks are filled with attractive illustrations and artistically presented content. Church materials should be equally appealing and educationally sound. Colorful workbooks, worthwhile handcrafts, and attractive visual aids should be expectations rather than exceptions. With effort, fresh new presentations can be given to solid biblical material.

Captivating

The program should flow smoothly from one activity to the next, giving variety, dimension, and involvement to class experiences. Sharing between students and teachers is important.

Teaching tips, source material, lesson plans, and daily assistance are built into the curriculum. These show teachers where they are going and how to get there. Each lesson needs a sense of freshness even though it builds on the learning of the previous day.

Conclusive

Lessons must build upon one another in a coherent, orderly fashion. The Bible truth taught daily should fit into an overall unit of learning that unfolds a yet larger theme as time progresses.

Age-appropriate activities should also be evident in the curriculum materials. A progression of Christian teaching should increase with higher grade levels.

Steps in Program Selection

The VBS planning committee must be sufficiently familiar with curriculum to make a wise choice. Several steps are involved in this process.

Survey Curriculum Options

Sample materials should be obtained. Usually preview kits are available for examination. These include a director's guide, teacher's guides, student materials, sample handcraft, and publicity items. Local Christian bookstores may feature a VBS display or hold a curriculum preview session where a variety of materials are exhibited and discussed.

Select Curriculum

The VBS planning committee should carefully examine the samples. Having narrowed the curriculum options to those which are educationally and theologically appropriate for their church, attention can be turned to economics.

The planning committee should use the "VBS Curriculum Evaluation Form" found in the *Instructor's Guide* for this course. Rarely will you discover the "perfect" VBS curriculum. Usually you will select a curriculum which meets your overall goals and presents the fewest problems.

Order Curriculum

Check Sunday School enrollment, past VBS enrollments, and results of neighborhood surveys (or other available outreach data) to determine the general amount of the most basic materials first. It is better to have too much than not enough, so add a reasonable number of extras when ordering. Check for return policies which may be allowed for unopened, unused materials. Order well in advance to avoid the risk of receiving materials late.

Examine the remaining budget. The teacher and student Bible study materials are not the best items for substitution, deletion, or donation. Refreshments, recreation, and craft supply purchases are more flexible.

Check Materials

Completeness and proper condition should be checked as soon as materials arrive. Do so before distribution to staff members. A complete inventory of all items ordered and received, distributions made, and a memo of storage locations should be kept.

Prepare Materials

The VBS director and the department heads should be briefed on the overall program to insure adequate preparation. They should study everything from the leader's guide through the handcrafts to understand how the overall theme fits together.

Actual preparation of materials should begin immediately after the briefing session so supplies for student projects and handcrafts are ready before VBS begins. How you distribute responsibilities will vary with the abilities of the staff. Perhaps you will need additional workers to help prepare handcrafts, allowing teachers more time for lesson preparation. A variety of groups or individuals can be involved in such projects—youth organizations, shut-ins, young mothers with home responsibilities, and senior citizens. The VBS program grows more interesting when people work together in teaching, preparing materials, giving, and praying.

Know Materials

Group leaders and other teaching staff should be encouraged to read the entire curriculum at one time. This gives an overview of the program. After this reading, there should be careful, critical study. The curriculum's purposes and the consistency of following them throughout the course must be re-evaluated so classroom aims are carried out effectively.

Use of the Bible should be generous. Study Scripture portions carefully, noting the context and related teachings. Passages should be prayerfully read, as the Holy Spirit makes them a reality. Experienced teachers may feel the lessons are quite basic and straightforward. Novice teachers, however, may require more study time. Reference books, suggested in the teacher's guide, can be borrowed from the library, or other teachers, for further insights. Obtain all necessary resource materials and teaching aids well in advance so there is ample time to become familiar with them.

A lesson plan for each school day with an outline of the intended teaching procedure should be prepared to delegate responsibilities among various workers. Memory activities, craft materials, recreation, and music should be listed so teachers can prepare them before VBS begins.

These preparations may be part of a training series. Teachers must still familiarize themselves with departmental materials and ready themselves for personal teaching responsibilities.

Summary

Curriculum materials determine the content and related experiences included in VBS. Bible Study, worship and evangelism, character building, Christian service, and fellowship are essential ingredients in VBS curriculum. To be effective, it should be complete, correlated, creative, child- and life-related, current, captivating, and conclusive. These factors will influence the planning committee's selection of materials. Proper curriculum orientation and preparation are necessary for VBS success.

For Further Discussion

1. How can the six basic areas of need be met at different age levels?
2. In what ways can teachers be relieved of the responsibility of preparing student handbooks and craft supplies?
3. Discuss ways to get fully acquainted with lesson material.

For Application

1. Secure VBS curriculum materials and evaluate them according to the standards presented in this chapter.
2. Outline a plan for thoroughly acquainting each VBS teacher with the curriculum materials selected.

Organizations Which Can Help

American Ministries/Intercom.
3739 Canyon Dr.
Rapid City, SD 57702
605-343-6064

Gospel Publishing House
  Radiant Life Curriculum
1445 Boonville Ave.
Springfield, MO 65802
417-831-8000

Augsburg Fortress Publishers
426 S. Fifth St. Box 1209
Minneapolis, MN 55440
800-328-4648 or 612-330-3300

Marketplace 29 AD
PO Box 29
Stevensville, MI 49127
800-345-29AD or 616-429-6442

Concording Publishing House
3558 S. Jefferson
St. Louis, MO 63118
314-268-1000

Standard Publishing
8121 Hamilton Ave.
Cincinnati, OH 45231
513-931-4050

David C. Cook Publishing Co.
850 N. Grove Rd.
Elgin, IL 60120
800-323-7543

WordAction Publication
PO Box 419527
Kansas City, MO 64141
800-877-0700

Gospel Light Publications
2300 Knoll Dr.
Ventura, CA 93003
800-4-GOSPEL

VBS
IMPLEMENTATION

4

The ministry of Vacation Bible School has benefited from a century of ideas contributed by multitudes of Christians exercising their spiritual gifts. Well-designed, modern curriculums have taken away much of the work necessary for this extensive project. However, time and effort from many dedicated individuals must still be invested for best results. To fully glorify God, every area of the VBS program needs careful supervision.

A prayerful search for the most qualified personnel is critical if the staff is to accomplish its goals and objectives. Planning and preparing remain lifeless details until energized by people who can work together as a team.

Stewardship

Over the last one hundred years, vast changes in the world and the lifestyles we lead have paralleled responsive changes in VBS. The needs of families have forced many of these changes. Due to crowded schedules, most churches have reduced VBS programs from two weeks to one. Two-income households brought about the evening school concept. The age of specialization changed the approach to personnel training. Economic changes have cancelled some schools, while others have rallied with creative solutions to stretch their funds and continue the evangelistic impact on their community. Presently, VBS addresses squarely the question, debated in society as well as in the church, of what priority should be given to the needs of children.

As VBS approaches the end of its first century of service, prudent use of time, talent, money, and facilities are more important than ever. Publishers recognize the financial strain on local congregations and continue to keep materials attractive and at the lowest possible cost. VBS publishers have also been generally responsive to customer service issues.

27

Prayer Support

The spiritual preparation of teachers, workers, and students is vital. Daily prayer for guidance and wisdom provides confidence that the Holy Spirit "will guide you into all the truth" (John 16:13). All personnel must draw on God's strength for their responsibilities. "He gives strength to the weary, and to him who lacks might He increases power" (Isa. 40:29). Schedule prayer together in the upcoming training sessions and, if possible, during the week of VBS.

Personnel

The variety of service opportunities keeps VBS an attractive test area for volunteers. However, growth in spiritual maturity is a primary requirement for all leadership positions. A VBS worker cannot be spiritually effective without a personal relationship with God. Indeed, the work of the Holy Spirit in the lives of students can only be accomplished through leaders who have a vital experience with Jesus Christ. The workers should be enthusiastic about sharing Christ with students.

Enlisting Personnel

Luke 6:12,13 suggests how Jesus recruited workers. He prayed about the selection of disciples. He chose workers to meet predetermined standards and then challenged them with the importance of their task. God's guidance in the search for workers is imperative.

Organizationally, the personnel needed will depend on the school's overall objective and the curriculum chosen to meet those goals. The first step in enlisting VBS personnel is to begin with the most productive sources from the previous year. Although educational requirements vary with the position, each worker needs to be adaptable to the age group with whom he or she has agreed to work.

Most curriculums will provide guidance in how to conduct your recruitment effort. Regardless of how the planning committee approaches the selection of staff, each volunteer should receive a follow-up contact from the leadership to clearly establish an understanding of his or her responsibilities. Most other apprehensions from volunteers can be settled during the orientation and training meetings. Enthusiasm for the program needs to be communicated early. Quickly show appreciation for the effort invested.

Supervising Personnel

Improving the effectiveness of personnel requires sensitivity to the people involved. Not only should individuals have a sense of accomplishment and satisfaction, but the church should feel a harmonious team spirit.

The development of good interpersonal relationships will help make VBS a positive experience for all involved. In large schools, born from large congregations, there may not be initial rapport between workers. The VBS director can be an encourager and morale-builder. The spiritual attitude of leaders sets the tone for the entire school. The pastor's active interest in VBS, and his support of the staff's ministry, do much to create a total team spirit. Even if he does not teach, his presence and encouraging words are appreciated. Active interest and participation from other church leaders will strengthen bonds between VBS and other ministries in the church.

Recognize Service
To unite VBS workers, set them apart for Christian service and enlist the cooperation of the entire congregation. A dedication service may be conducted prior to opening the school. A charge from the pastor will clearly demonstrate the impact of VBS as *ministry*. Public and personal recognition of the VBS staff need not be deferred to a closing program.

Training Volunteers
Effective training determines the success of a VBS program. Both group and individual instruction are essential. The curriculum of choice will guide most training in regards to orientation of a specific theme and publicity of the overall program.

- The leadership will need to take responsibility for training personnel in topics pertinent to their school.
- Perhaps a specific missions emphasis will need to be explained thoroughly.
- Details about transportation and safety may be a concern.
- If music is a key feature, you may want to devote time to learning it together.
- Sufficient time should be spent discussing how to lead a child to Christ.

The appointed VBS director is the most likely person to lead the training sessions, or at least to coordinate the effort.

Equipment and Supplies
Basic equipment such as chalkboards, bulletin boards, audio-visual support, musical instruments, tables and chairs of proper sizes for the various age groups may already be provided in the rooms. Other conveniences such as wastebaskets, glue, pencils, scissors, art supplies and tools may be needed. Recreation supplies and a first aid kit should be readily available to the staff. Conduct an additional thorough reading of the curriculum materials for the explicit purpose of listing supplies and equipment needed.

If someone has been recruited to supervise acquisition of equipment and supplies, set a deadline for all workers to submit lists of what they need. Delegation of this task to a central purchasing or acquisition agent saves both time and money. Purchases can be made in bulk. Confusion over borrowed or donated items is reduced. The entire church may want to get involved through designated "bring-a-supply" Sundays which can reinforce publicity and unity.

Devote storage space to collection of supplies and equipment for VBS. Be sure the location for donated items is clear to the donors. Coordinate usage of large equipment and facilities with other ministries of the church or community location.

Transportation

Although many teachers and students make their own transportation arrangements, the VBS planning committee should appoint someone to determine transportation needs and ways to meet them. Inquiry can be made during pre-registration. Once the needs are discovered, they can be charted on a community map and transportation routes determined. A church van or bus, car pools, or public transportation can cover the routes.

Properly licensed vehicles and competent drivers, each with adequate insurance coverage, are necessary. Runs should start early enough to cover the route without a feeling of tension or need for haste.

In all transportation matters from boarding and exiting vehicles to locking doors and fastening seat belts, every safety measure should be observed. Overcrowding of cars, buses, and vans must be avoided. Create proper conditions for the driver. It is helpful to have crossing guards stationed at corners near the church and to designate a special section of the parking lot for the pick-up and discharge of students.

Enrollment

Again, the larger the VBS the more sophisticated will be the enrollment effort. Some publishers offer materials for nursery through adult while others provide only for children's departments but suggest auxiliary courses for youth and adults. Enrollment efforts may differ for each group. Providing a nursery may be an attraction to adults wanting to attend class themselves.

There are five major sources for enrollment: present Sunday School attendees, former VBS attendees, neighborhood contacts, friends, and community publicity. If these contacts are developed and strengthened, encouraging results will follow.

Both Sunday School and VBS records provide lists of potential students. Those who have attended Sunday School or a previous VBS know what to expect and are more likely to accept an invitation to attend.

Neighborhood families may be hesitant if they are unfamiliar with the church. However, this can be overcome by penetrating the immediate area surrounding the church with early publicity and inviting whole families to participate. Excitement for VBS can be added by holding a special event prior to opening.

Opening day runs smoothly when specially-trained workers have developed a means to readily identify those pre-registered and efficiently handle newcomers. VBS curriculum developers are extremely helpful to offer supplies and guidance in record keeping.

Preparing for Opening Day

Preparations should be completed at least a day before VBS opens. Rooms should be set up the day before, if at all possible, so everything is in place for the opening. Each class should be equipped with all the needed materials not already distributed. Extra supplies should be accessible if the anticipated enrollment is exceeded.

The director should check last-minute details with key assistants. Transportation plans need to be finalized. Attendance record forms should be ready for distribution early on opening day. Registration procedures should be clearly understood by those who enroll students. The kitchen crew should have a refreshment distribution plan.

Attendees quickly sense a staff's preparedness, or lack of it. They sense the freedom of a teacher who has spent enough time in preparation to freely interact with students. Indeed, attitudes formed the first day have a lasting impression; they influence behavior during the rest of VBS.

Summary

Preparation energizes planning ideas. Careful preparation in stewardship, prayer support, personnel, training, equipment and supplies, transportation, and enrollment make for a successful opening day. As the church bathes these preparations in prayer, God's blessings on VBS will be evident.

Enlisting personnel requires knowing how to discover and motivate workers. Training includes spiritual readiness as well as organizational procedures. Everyone has a special responsibility to fulfill. The carefully chosen and trained staff will be able to effectively communicate the good news of the gospel.

For Further Discussion

1. How would a study of age characteristics help a teacher?
2. Discuss proper and improper ways to approach individuals about serving in VBS.
3. What methods can be used to motivate a staff's involvement in a training program?

4. How can enrollment be handled so that it does not disrupt the school?
5. What is the most effective way to group children in VBS?
6. Discuss ways to organize prayer support for VBS.

For Application

1. Plan a dedication service for VBS staff which could be used prior to the school's opening.
2. Prepare job descriptions for key VBS positions.
3. Estimate the potential enrollment of a VBS for your church citing the sources used for your conclusions.
4. Work out a complete listing of equipment and supplies needed for one VBS department of twenty students.

Organizations Which Can Help

See also Chapter Three Curriculum Publishers.

Bible Games Company
403 Gaskin Ave.
PO Box 272
Gambier, OH 43022

Shining Star Publications
1204 Buchanan St. Box 299
Carthage, IL 62321-0299

VBS PROBLEM SOLVING

5

People working closely together, often in less than ideal situations, will usually face some problems; from the simple to the complex. Busy schedules leave little time to solve them. However, with advance planning, preparation, and prayer, many problems can be prevented. When leaders and committees plan together, some difficult areas can be foreseen and alternate procedures arranged.

Seeking the Lord's guidance and blessing upon VBS is a natural part of church life. The entire church family needs to uphold the VBS program, staff, and attenders before the Lord. For the most part, administrative problems can be worked out long before VBS begins. Difficulties with students are less predictable, particularly large numbers of unfamiliar children. Unknown factors, such as irregular attendance and behavior problems, cause the most concern. Problems that arise in such areas must be dealt with promptly and effectively.

Attendance

While an attractive, personalized invitation, saturated with prayer, can move hearts to respond, the decision to attend rests with the individual. Once enrolled, continued attendance can be encouraged by the teacher.

Since VBS is brief, it is important the teacher establish warm personal relationships with students from the first day. Teachers should learn names and individual interests as quickly as possible. Those who sense friendship and concern will want to return. Opportunities to talk about topics of importance will continue to encourage participation. Personal rapport also enables the teacher to gain insights about the individual and the teaching/learning situation. Informal moments during pre-session, recreation, refreshment break, and craft time are opportunities to get better acquainted. These times may prove to be more valuable than any other contact.

33

Involving participants in a well-planned daily program to discover God's truth helps stabilize attendance. If one day's knowledge obviously contributes to the next, the importance of consistent participation will be recognized. The more relevant Bible content is to the student, the greater the motivation to attend. An installment approach to special service projects provides incentive to return as well.

Assigning students specific responsibilities may also help involvement. Children, for example, generally want to help arrange tables and chairs, distribute and put away supplies, serve refreshments, operate audiovisual equipment, lead in prayer, and run errands. Youth and adults will rally around a common project or interest.

The program itself should attract people. Appearance in everything from publicity items to day-to-day supplies should be attractive and communicate enjoyment. A lively pace to all the activities, without rushing, will keep the anticipation level high. Appealing music and other meaningful features will help accomplish this also.

Besides the intrinsic motivation to attend a VBS, extra incentives may be offered. Most VBS curriculum publishers have a wide range of items which correspond to the overall theme. Contests and fairs are effective in some areas. Offering bigger and better awards each year must be avoided if these incentives are to be maintained in a proper perspective. Another problem with contests is that someone must lose. It is difficult to assess the time and effort an individual puts into achieving a goal. Rewards, therefore, should recognize everyone's effort.

In spite of program planning, good teaching, and teacher-student relationships, absenteeism will occur. In spite of the best efforts, some people find it difficult to relate to strange situations or unfamiliar people. Events outside the control of leadership may be a factor; such as family trips, illness, oversleeping, or circumstances at home. At times, other scheduled events cannot be avoided; such as swimming lessons, community programs, or a doctor's appointment. These preemptions to the VBS program can be disheartening to workers who have invested tremendous effort in preparation. A wise director will prepare the staff for these inevitable events and circumvent the disheartened volunteer.

If possible, direct communication helps ascertain a reason for the absence. Regardless of the reason, contact with the student should be attempted. A follow-up system, often a non-threatening telephone call, can show interest in a caring home-church relationship.

Starting a program promptly on time helps discourage tardiness. Punctuality can also be rewarded. When tardiness is habitual or disruptive, a polite, simple instruction should be offered. If the offender is a child, direct the communication to the home. A telephone call may even clarify starting time or discern an unexpected difficulty in transportation or parking.

Discipline

Often discipline is thought of as punishment when a child misbehaves. Actually, discipline is something done *for* and *with* anyone whose behavior is offensive or inconsiderate to others. Discipline is training which corrects and guides the individual as he progresses from external control by parents, teachers, or other authority figures to self-control and guidance by the Holy Spirit. Some people require a great deal of external control to benefit from group experiences while others have reached a point of fairly reliable self-control and can function happily within a looser framework. The VBS staff should attempt to identify causes for misbehavior and seek ways to encourage positive actions that help everyone develop into Spirit-guided, self-controlled individuals.

Identifying Misbehavior

While a child may not know why he acts the way he does, the volunteer worker needs to attempt identification of the cause. This identification helps the teacher to know who is the proper authority to handle the situation. Simple classroom misconduct, typical of most children, can be handled with the age characteristic training the teacher received prior to VBS. The teacher should first examine his attitudes toward the child. Verify the teaching to be spiritually prepared, relevant to needs, and exemplified in the teacher's life.

Second, the teacher examines the classroom environment. Improper seating, unnecessary distractions, or inadequate supplies can impede the creation of a learning environment where children know each other and interact in a happy, friendly atmosphere.

Third, consider elements of the child's life outside VBS. Perhaps the home environment might make him seek special attention. It may be that a permissive atmosphere prevails at home so the child has difficulty controlling himself in a group. Those actions which seem unacceptable at VBS may result from expressions of speech, habits, apathy, or a lack of reverence found at home. Detection of these problems are often uncovered by the classroom teacher. Resolution may require the intervention of the VBS director working closely with the church's pastoral staff. Some churches have specific guidelines in place for conduct intervention. Observe these at all times. Volunteers should not be expected to perform as trained social workers, therapists, or child psychologists/counselors.

Finally, before calling professionals to intervene, study the student to see how he reacts in group situations. Odd behavior, inconsistent with other actions, may be momentary thoughtlessness to gain attention or to express boredom with materials that lack challenge. Whatever the case when dealing with problems, people, *especially children*, need an extra portion of Christian love and understanding.

The circumstances and people involved in each problem situation must be examined as objectively as possible. When this is done, causes of the problem can often be alleviated or completely removed.

Encourage a Positive Atmosphere

To set the proper atmosphere, expect positive behavior and commend it when it is present. At the same time, establish authority kindly, but firmly, from the start. Once the entire staff agrees upon boundaries of conduct and goals of the program, each teacher should set and explain ground rules appropriate to the class. The number of rules should be limited to avoid confusing and frustrating students. In some cases, particularly with teenagers and adult groups, students themselves may even formulate their own guidelines. In any event, teachers should work together as a team to maintain positive behavior.

When problems are handled lovingly but firmly, students sense genuine concern. Love promotes positive behavior and satisfies needs. Prayer for God's guidance and blessing upon every decision is also an essential ingredient in discipline.

Challenging Situations

When an overwhelming response in attendance is the result of promotion efforts, rapid reorganization is necessary. Accept the situation as the tremendous opportunity it is and do not panic. Unrealistic student-teacher ratios need not be the demise of the program. Capitalize on the desire of most older students to help themselves, and encourage them to do as much a possible before seeking assistance. Cooperative efforts of small groups and teamwork should be praised.

With younger children, it is essential to locate additional helpers when enrollment is too large. Some mature teenagers or untapped adults may volunteer their services on a rotating basis. A general plan of action should be agreed upon in advance. If a young child becomes overwhelmed with the situation and uncontrollably distraught, advise the parent immediately.

First Aid

If an illness or accident occurs during VBS, immediately contact the parent or initiate emergency medical procedures. It is now commonplace for local ordinances to mandate certain criteria for large assemblies of people, regardless of the nature or sponsoring agency. It will be important to the present witness of the church and feasibility of future events that the regulations be adhered to respectfully. Attenders and their families will also appreciate your thoughtfulness.

Special Education

Recent years have also seen a greater awareness for people with special needs. The mentally handicapped need special care-givers. The physically challenged need greater access to events. The intellectually gifted require additional stimulation. It is good to remember the example Jesus stated in Matthew 19:13-15. The receptive attitude, personified by children, is exactly the condition required to accept faith in Jesus Christ and is the goal of the gospel.

People and problems seem to go together, but the promise of the Lord is with those who faithfully minister in VBS. "Then the word of the Lord came to Jeremiah, saying, 'Behold, I am the Lord, the God of all flesh; is anything too difficult for Me?'" (Jer. 32:26,27).

Summary

Careful planning and preparation will help a teacher avoid most problems which may arise in VBS. Difficulties with irregular attendance are not predictable, but they are manageable. The staff can do much to create an atmosphere which discourages problems.

Attendance is promoted by the personal love and concern of teachers, student involvement, effective programming, and occasionally extra incentives. Absentees should be contacted personally and encouraged to return. Starting VBS promptly with an interesting opening discourages tardiness.

Discipline should help students move from external control to self-control and guidance by the Holy Spirit. Identifying the causes of misconduct helps develop a framework for favorable behavior. Positive expectations, love, and staff teamwork contribute to this model.

For Further Discussion

1. How can VBS develop self-discipline?
2. What is the relationship of leadership characteristics to behavioral problems?
3. Use open-ended stories or role play to illustrate discipline problems, and then discuss possible solutions.

For Application

1. Prepare a list of useful incentives for VBS based on suggestions in books, supply catalogs, or VBS materials.
2. Compare VBS attendance records in a least three schools. Seek to determine what each school did to encourage attendance and whether there was a pattern of attendance.

PROMOTING SUMMER MINISTRIES

6

Church and community people need to be informed of the unique opportunity summer ministries brings to hear and study the Word of God. How can they know of this unless someone is distributing information about summer ministries? The importance of promotion cannot be overestimated. Publicity projects an image of your summer programming which will influence the success of the entire season. All advance preparations will bear fruit only if people attend.

Plan for Promotion

The summer planning committee should delegate publicity responsibilities early. In this way a separate committee can devote itself to ways of making program plans known to your church and community.

Establish Committee

The size of the publicity committee will vary according to the needs of the programs and the number of qualified persons available. Committee members are needed who have an understanding of communication principles:
- working well with people
- writing ability
- art and graphic design
- creativity
- willingness to work.

Plan Program

While the publicity committee is responsible for planning a promotion schedule, the methods to be used, and the people to involve, these proposals must be submitted to the program planning committee for approval and allocation of funds before action can be taken.

A good promotion schedule outlines week-by-week plans for publicizing summer ministries. You will normally need to allow several months to prepare your publicity and six to eight weeks in which to impact the various groups and individuals you have targeted. The methods used will vary with needs and available resources. The committee can extend itself by involving groups and individuals in promotional activities. For example, Sunday School departments can participate in a poster-making contest while older children distribute literature in the community. Maximum involvement in promotion often produces maximum interest and concern in the school itself.

Steps in Promotion

Effective promotion does not depend on the number of novel ideas invented, but on the care with which the vital steps in promotional planning are followed.

Identify Target Group

Objectives, set by the planning committee, will help to determine the potential summer audience. If your programs are to be primarily educational, the target group will probably be those in the church. If your programs are to be strongly evangelistic, the target group more likely will be in the community. Attention must be focused on the people to be reached through the ministry.

Select Media

Select appropriate media to reach the target group and to accomplish objectives. All possible media should be considered.
- Are newspaper, radio, and television available?
- What would their impact be on the target group?
- Which methods of direct or personal contact would be effective with the target group?
  - neighborhood saturation
  - door-to-door canvass
  - individual contact
  - telephone brigade
- What types of indirect contact would work best?
  - posters
  - yard signs
  - billboards
  - direct mailings

The promotion committee needs to consider all possible ideas for reaching the target group before deciding upon a specific plan of action.

Plan Effectively

The message is as important as the way it is presented. Together they must capture the attention and interest of those to be reached.

What will excite the children, teens, and adults in your community so they will want to attend?

The proper format increases the power of the message. News about your summer schedule in the paper can be a paid advertisement, an article for the church page, or a feature story. Regardless of which is used, the message must be understandable and clearly present what will take place.

Everything produced must be top quality. Good writing style is essential. Art work, photography, and graphics must be well done. Professional work is not necessary but an attractive, neat, informative product is within the range of most churches' capabilities.

Provide a Response Mechanism

After the target group is identified, media selected, and message determined, provision for response is needed. A pre-registration form to complete, a phone number to call, a ticket, or a coupon to return can be provided. If people are to respond, it must be as convenient and painless as possible.

Pray Expectantly

Promotional planning should be kept before the Lord in prayer since sincere prayer, with a desire to please God, accomplishes much. "If you ask Me anything in My name, I will do it" (John 14:14). "All things are possible to him who believes" (Mark 9:23). The praying church needs to be kept informed as it supports VBS. Through prayer, God can prepare the hearts of the staff and those who will attend.

Phases of Promotion

Promotion includes three phases: advance, in-progress, and follow-up. While the majority of details are completed before summer ministry programs begin, some features need attention during and after.

Advance Promotion

Recruitment, progress reports, and target emphasis are the major thrusts of advance promotion. Initial responsibilities are making known to the congregation any needs of a given program and emphasizing recruitment. Opportunities for service can be presented to adults and older youth in the congregation through a variety of methods.

Progress concerning up-to-date needs, staff who have been appointed, training schedules, and the pre-registration information continue to build awareness. These reports help increase the congregation's personal involvement. As a result, the announcement of dates, time, and themes—an important feature of early promotion—has more significance.

The greatest amount of promotional effort, though, should be concentrated on those who might attend. Publicity focuses on those within the church family and the community who make up the target group. It informs them of program details, transportation provisions, and other helpful information. Set dates by which emphases, such as recruitment, are to be met and write them on a promotion calendar.

In-progress Promotion

The congregation must be informed of progress during the summer. Facts and figures about enrollment and attendance should be shared with those who support the programs with their finances, supplies, and prayers. They should be informed of achievements and problems, requesting continued prayer support. Invitations to attend closing events should be given to all interested individuals.

Continued outreach can be promoted during the programs. Word-of-mouth publicity by attendees often increases attendance during the course of ongoing events. A special mid-season event, such as a picnic, helps increase interest. Pictures and a newspaper article about activities will keep the church before the community.

The events and their results should be preserved through photographs, slides, and/or video tape. These can be publicly presented and copies kept for next year's publicity committee.

Follow-up Promotion

All materials, such as posters, banners, and circulars that were used in your promotion effort should be removed from the church and other sites as soon as events are over.

The main responsibility of follow-up promotion is to present a final report of statistics and results to the congregation. The church bulletin or a pulpit announcement can be used to accomplish this.

If a mid-year rally or reunion is planned, the publicity committee is to be responsible for communication. Publicity would be on a much smaller scale, primarily directed to those who attended the summer programs.

Types of Promotion

The promotion of summer ministries can be as varied and interesting as your imagination and creativity allow. It is essential that publicity be attractive and appealing to those being reached. All publicity should be absolutely truthful since the programs must live up to advertising claims. Church literature, mailings, mass media, and personal contacts are widely-used methods. They can be adapted to individual situations or act as a catalyst for creative alternatives.

Church Literature

Use every audio and visual device possible to enthuse the congregation. Written announcements or inserts in the church bulletin should include dates, time, theme, and special features. Workers and highlights of various summer programs may be listed. Interesting testimonies from those who participated last year should be featured. Those who found Christ as a result of a summer ministry program, or those who are anticipating this year's ministry, are excellent sources. Verbal announcements from the pulpit, at midweek service, and in Sunday School should be made. A skit, an interview, or a pantomime adds dramatic impact. Posters, banners, displays, indoor and outdoor signs keep the summer ministries visually before the people. When this enthusiasm is generated in the church, it can overflow to every corner of the community.

Mailings

Direct mail is an effective means of notifying people about programs. Letters or postcards should be sent to last year's attendees. The mailing list may be expanded to include all families enrolled in other programs of the church. Brochures attractively presenting the basic information can be sent bulk mail. The monthly church letter can also be used to acquaint and inform the church family of ministry needs and progress in addition to more detailed pre-registration information.

Mass Media

Most newspapers regularly provide a church page for special church announcements. Often a newspaper will run a news release or even a feature article. Acceptable news stories answer the usual journalistic questions: Who? What? Where? When? Why? How? Features are longer, more informative, and human-interest centered.

Local papers are often willing to publish the names of community members involved in events and activities. Therefore, names of key staff with pictures of a few individuals involved with the program are helpful. Action photos, such as registering several children or a chairman explaining a display to the pastor, are especially interesting to local newspapers.

It may be possible to obtain permission from community authorities to mount a public address system on a car or van, and drive through the community announcing your event while distributing literature, balloons, or buttons. Some radio and television stations carry local news items without charge. Others sell or give time for spot announcements of a civic or religious nature. Some merchants will display posters.

Parade

A parade is also an excellent way to promote a summer program. Choose a theme and invite all who are interested to march. It is most effective if the parade is scheduled a few days before the opening. The route should be worked out ahead of time and have the approval of the police and other municipal officials. In some communities, you may be able to receive an escort by the police or fire department.

Children can decorate bicycles, teens and adults can decorate cars or pick-up trucks. The addition of a marching band would be great but a vehicle equipped with a sound system and a loudspeaker playing marching music will work, too.

Be sure to tell your local newspapers and television news departments about the event. You may be pleasantly surprised at the positive coverage your parade can receive. If no one from the media chooses to cover your event, be sure to have your own photographer present to record it. You may be able to get the pictures in a local paper. Even if no one will run them, you will have some great shots to use in your publicity next year!

Personal Contact

Even with use of every form of mass media, personal contact must not be neglected. The vast majority of people who visit your church for the first time will be there primarily through the influence of a neighbor, close friend, or family member. Encourage church members to talk about the benefits of your summer ministries to friends, neighbors, store clerks, and everyone else they come in contact with. Extra pre-registration forms can be handed out to contacts.

A phone brigade could be organized using people who effectively communicate over the phone. Pamphlets and information can be distributed at neighborhood playgrounds, parks, and shopping plazas as well as during a house-to-house canvass. Local restrictions with regard to distributing literature should be observed.

Making personal contacts is a ministry in itself. Those doing it should be prepared to respond with wisdom and tact to spiritual needs that may be revealed. If it is not possible to help personally, reference to qualified sources should be given.

Creative Ideas

A good imagination can conceive of many ingenious promotional methods. Balloons, buttons, bumper stickers, puppets, contests, and a booth at a local fair are but a few possible interest-catchers.

Summary

An effective publicity program is an essential part of overall program planning. The publicity committee, appointed by the planning committee, determines the methods, schedule, and persons involved in promotional efforts. Steps in publicity include: identify the target group(s), select media, plan effectively, provide a response system, and pray expectantly. Each of these steps must keep the initial objectives in mind.

Publicity efforts before each event begins involve recruitment, progress reports, and target emphasis. Progress reports, continued outreach, and preservation of highlights all require attention. A final report, and perhaps a mid-year summer ministries event, are handled later by the committee.

Church publicity, mailings, mass media, personal contacts, and creative ideas can be used to acquaint the church family and community with the merits of summer ministries. Possibilities for effective promotion are innumerable. Be creative!

For Further Discussion

1. How can specific information about a target group be gathered?
2. In your community, what types of media are most effective for promotion?
3. Discuss an appropriate calendar for the various phases of promotion.

For Application

1. Write a brief news item about some phase of a summer program using an approach that would appeal to your community.
2. Plan promotion for a summer ministry program which would be held in your church facilities.

Organizations Which Can Help

Vision Graphics (clip art)
PO Box 494
South Plainfield, NJ 07080

Weber Photo Productions
(promotional pieces)
PO Box 1929
Fort Collins, CO 80522

SUMMER MINISTRIES CURRICULUM

7

Beyond mere promotion of any church program, there must be a sense of vision for ground-breaking efforts. Summer can, and should, be used as a valuable and necessary period to cultivate relationships. With experience, the ministries of summer will be anxiously anticipated for the spiritual refreshment they provide.

A novice spiritual planter, on virgin soil, should devote more time, at first, to preparing the ground than sowing the seed. The first summer set aside for "something new" may not seem to be your most productive. Each successive season will reap a more bountiful harvest.

Adaptability is the underpinning of any curriculum design when the number of workers and participants will vary from session to session as is so typical in the summer months. This is understandable given the multiple summer opportunities a community may offer. You will be in competition for the attention of everyone involved. Program leaders soon realize there is no *one* curriculum sufficient to meet the needs of all age groups. Volunteer workers should use flexible methods and creatively mix and match compatible materials.

Perhaps the most bewildering portion of summer ministry leadership comes with the question "What will we do in addition to VBS?" An exciting and innovative Vacation Bible School can leave other programs longing for refreshment. Choosing curriculum materials, beyond VBS, requires some attention to the purpose in which they will be used.

Children's Ministries

Take a Break

It is often a welcome change to incorporate more exciting, student-involved approaches into other established programs. There may have been more activities in the VBS curriculum than you were able to utilize during the regular VBS session. Try

47

reinforcing those themes with the extra activities and crafts at established Sunday School or Children's Church times. Perhaps you may have enough materials to conduct a Backyard Bible Club in a neighborhood that needs additional attention.

Sunday School

As the vacation season opens, a marked drop in attendance may occur. Travel schedules, of workers and students alike, may destroy an otherwise workable structure. Summer can be a good time to explore alternative teaching styles and curriculum. Another Vacation Bible School curriculum may be adaptable to a Sunday to Sunday structure. David C. Cook's *Very Exciting Bible School* series is designed with reproducible activity sheets. Other suggestions are included for rotating teachers from one age group to another, using the one prepared lesson. Children can be rotated to a different center each Sunday. Whether a church is large or small, a little creativity and willingness to break form can bring a whole new dimension to the Sunday School hour. The children will enjoy the experience and the leaders will not sacrifice the instructional purposes of the Sunday School ministry.

Children's Church

A similar departure in form may be welcomed by the worship hour workers. Summer may be a excellent time to investigate materials from a different publisher. The summer attendees can be viewed as a focus group while the workers explore their talents. Children's worship materials are constantly being revised. If you have not used a publisher for some time, you may want to obtain current materials and see how things have changed. You will find more colorful visuals, multi-media activities, and exciting music have all been added. A more coordinated effort in applying the worship preferences of the adult services has been the motivation of most publishers.

The purpose of meaningful worship need not be lost with change. If you are in an area where the summer children's worship program would otherwise need to be suspended, the summer months may be the time to cultivate new volunteers who can only commit to one month at a time. Choose materials with four-part series and assign a fresh team to each month. You may also test three new curriculums before the crush of fall crowds return to the classroom.

Curriculum Development

Perhaps your idea of a break is writing original lessons. You may have longed for a specific topic to be addressed or a different teaching approach to be explored. Summer is a good time to experiment with your creativity.

Secure the appropriate permissions of the church leadership and examine publisher catalogs and review kits. The end of this chapter lists several organizations with materials you should analyze. Begin in a manageable fashion. Decide on a format you would like to develop, age group or audience you want to target, and the teaching method, or collection of methods, you want to emphasize.

Determine if you want to create a single lesson or a series. Following the basic structure of a curriculum you admire is recommended. Be faithful to the purposes of the program with which you are working. Outline your material to serve as a checklist of important components to your presentation.

Seek the Lord's guidance from beginning to end and thank Him for all you will learn from the exercise. You will acquire a new appreciation for curriculum developers and you may discover a whole new ministry for yourself.

Youth Ministries

Teenagers and young adults can do more with the summer months than recreate or hold summer jobs. You can build a successful curriculum approach around activities they enjoy in the context of meeting their spiritual needs. Relationship building is extremely important for this age group. Idleness also provides the most opportunity for problems. Analyze what teenagers in your area are doing with their vacation time and design a curriculum to address the situation.

If your teens spend time in video arcades, create a youth center in an adjacent building to the church property or some other safe place. Make it attractive enough so they will want to bring their friends.

If your teens are enthralled with the film industry, develop a series of video nights. Video rentals are available from many Christian bookstores as well as public libraries, which cover a variety of positive, upbuilding topics. Provide refreshments and allow the conversation to naturally lead to discussions of Christian values.

Adolescence is a battle for identity. Combat the loss of community by providing service projects as opportunities for young people to contribute to the neighborhood and to caring for one another. Destructiveness is often the result of suppressed problems. As adolescents participate in the projects, leaders can guide them toward more openness and address classic questions of abuse, forgiveness, loneliness, peer pressure, phobias, school, or spiritual matters.

Young Adults

As older teens and young adults approach college and career choices, the thought of summer can bring about deep anxieties.

Employment and finances create all-time highs for stressful living. There can be a ministry in stress management to this age group. Guidance from mentors in vocational fields or educational counselors can provide much-needed quality time in conversation.

Organize a series of brunches, brown-bag seminars, or even casual coffee breaks to connect people with others in similar situations. Church leaders can provide information about summer internships for many vocations in addition to opportunities in the church itself.

Perhaps college-level instructors are among the members of your congregation. If so, they are likely candidates to help organize educational counseling services. Organize scouting trips to campuses where young adults can explore their possibilities for enrollment. You will be able to capture their natural spirit for adventure and help them build valuable peer relationships.

Despair and loneliness may be isolating many young adults in your community. Issues must be faced for which their parents cannot lend a voice of experience. Societal changes have rapidly created new choices never before considered. Develop forums for young adults to share their opinions and biblical options for lifestyle development. Often the support and reassurance of a trusted relationship will turn a life around.

Adults

Singles ministries are growing at phenomenal rates. These programs target all ages who, for a variety of reasons, are not supported by the companionship of a spouse. It is estimated that 51% of unchurched adults in America are single. What a mission field! These adults mostly need an opportunity to reinforce relationships with other adults battling the same life issues—not a matchmaking ministry.

Leadership Training

Summer may be a time to set apart a small group of workers who have demonstrated a spiritual gift for administration or teaching. You will want to capture the fresh context of their recent months of service by offering a leadership training course. Assess the amount of time available for this purpose and prepare training materials accordingly.

For general leadership development, the ETA *Classroom Series* titles fit conveniently into a quarter system. You may consider offering an adult elective through your Sunday School hour and select the ETA course title most helpful to your present volunteers. Alternate study methods allow for instruction through audio cassettes, video, or one-day seminars.

Examine the catalog or order blank of publishers you are presently using to see if other leadership training options are available.

These will generally be program specific but will coordinate nicely with the regular curriculum. Particularly if you have programs that recess for the summer months, you may want to keep your volunteers interested in the ministry while they rejuvenate their skills.

Summary

In contemplating summer ministry materials do not wait for a marketing campaign to come along beckoning "use me this summer." Rather, honestly determine the needs of your people to seek to apply materials, or help from organizations, that address that need.

Regular programs can be revitalized by experimenting with new and creative teaching methods. Do not overlook creative uses of unused Vacation Bible School materials in the context of other programs.

Each age group should be analyzed to determine if program voids exist. Closing down programs for the summer may do more harm than good. When a shortage of workers or other factors of program structure have prompted a hiatus, use the time as a relationship building venture. Materials that are adaptable to many cultures, church sizes, or budgets are available.

For Further Discussion

1. What programs in your church either scale down or shut down for the summer months? Are there other options which could work better in your situation this coming summer?
2. What age groups or specific interest groups are not currently being ministered to in your church during the summer months?
3. In addition to VBS, what have been the most successful summer ministries which have been in your church?

For Application

1. Make a list of all the curriculum materials (and their publishers) used in the Christian education ministries of your church. When was the last time these materials have been reviewed and compared with those from other publishers? What is your church's policy on curriculum reviews and selection?
2. Do an inventory of unused or partially used curriculum materials in your church. List several ways these materials could be incorporated into your summer ministries program.

Organizations Which Can Help

Charisma Life Publishers
K.I.D.S. Church
190 N. Westmonte Dr.
Altamonte Springs, FL 32714

Positive Action For Christ
PO Box 1948
Rocky Mount, NC 27801-1948

Focus on the Family Resources
Colorado Springs, CO 80995

SAM Journal
 (Single Adult Ministries)
PO Box 62056
Colorado Sprgs., CO 80962-2056

Group Books
PO Box 481
Loveland, CO 80539

Scripture Memory Fellowship
PO Box 24551
St. Louis, MO 63141

Ministries Today
PO Box 1615
Riverton, NJ 08077

Youth for Christ/USA
PO Box 228822
Denver, CO 80222

The Navigators
PO Box 6000
Colorado Springs, CO 80934

Youth Specialties
1224 Greenfield Dr.
El Cajon, CA 92021

DENOMINATIONALLY INSPIRED PROGRAMS

8

Around the turn of the century, the term *evangelical* came into vogue. It was understood to mean the collection of Christians, from Protestant groups, who would characterize their worship traditions as "conservative" or "fundamentalist." Under the broad collection of evangelicals, *denominations* organize multiple congregations legally, administratively, and theologically.

Evangelicalism, therefore, is not a single denomination, but a category of groups who share the commonality of basic doctrines. The practices, or implementation of doctrine into daily life, may vary among denominations. An urgency to share the gospel of Jesus Christ is common to all.

It is through the sharing of the gospel that Christian education programs are born. As one person, one church, or one denomination discovers a successful approach to faith development, it is often shared with appreciation among evangelicals. Since the time of the Reformation, a personal relationship to God has radically effected both the church and society. Historical documents record notable individuals who have contributed profoundly to Christian leadership as an outcome of their experiences with a denomination. Admittedly, some of those experiences were negative. Many more were positive.

Evangelical Training Association is but one of many parachurch organizations who have enjoyed a rich heritage of cooperation with dozens of denominations. Cooperation in this way helps broaden the world view of all participating churches and denominations. Parachurch organizations are also a way for participating churches to demonstrate the spiritual unity of the church. This is one manifestation of what Christ prayed for in John 17, "Holy Father, keep them in Thy name, the name which Thou hast given Me, that they may be one, even as We are" (v. 11b).

While some denominations grope for identity, others are thriving and can inspire us all with their creativity. Many denominations are open to sharing their curriculum materials with other smaller groups or local congregations. Some aggressively market to outside groups. As stated in previous chapters, summer may be the time for your local church to be inspired toward new or different communication methods. Loyalty to one's denomination is not to be questioned. Rather, seek the Lord's wisdom and vision for your own group when reviewing the program profiles of other denominations. "Therefore encourage one another, and build up one another, just as you also are doing" (1 Thess. 5:11).

Advocate Press
(Pentecostal Holiness Church)
P.O. Box 9, Franklin Springs, GA 30639-0009

New Converts: As people are won to the Lord, a nurturing process must take place. Often new believers feel overwhelmed and long for a systematic approach to spiritual growth. *First Things First, Foundations of the Faith for New Believers*, by Russell A. Board, is developed as thirteen basic Bible study lessons. The approach is easily adapted to a quarter study system. The material is presented in a small three-ring binder, making it easy to add study notes and related materials.

Handiness is an important factor when motivating good study habits. Each chapter briefly discusses basic doctrines of the church, citing Scripture references, and providing question and answer sections. Each lesson closes with a section titled "For Further Study" and provides space for the participant to record responses to key questions and Bible passages as the topic is explored throughout the week.

Many churches are finding this structure workable for a variety of topics or small groups needing guided instruction. Evangelical Training Association encourages church-designed courses for the unique doctrinal study or specific mission of denominations or local churches.

Board of C.E. of Church of God
(Church of God, Anderson)
Box 2458, Anderson, IN 46018-2458

Family Life: We read about the present threat to the institution of family, we witness injustices toward children and question the future of our society because we do not cherish our youth. Here is a denomination that actively chose to do something about it. *Believe The Children* was organized as a National Conference on Ministry to Children and Families. As might be expected in a conference format, notable plenary speakers were chosen, topical workshops organized, and exhibits were set up to display up-to-date resources. One evening, however, was devoted to a festival celebrating children. Area churches hosted the finale of this three-day event by opening its classrooms on Sunday morning to observe the methods of the experts put to task.

Conferences are a major undertaking but enormously beneficial to lay workers who otherwise would not have a source of encouragement, do not have a source to examine new materials or a way to gain insights from experienced leaders in ministry.

CRC Publications
(Christian Reformed)
2850 Kalamazoo Ave. S.E., Grand Rapids, MI 49560

Interfaith Women's Bible Study: Originally an experiment at a local church, "Coffee Break" ministries are now held across the denomination. Women are encouraged to bring their friends, share light refreshment over coffee, and open God's Word to discuss relevant topics of concern to all. A structured preschool children's program, conducted simultaneously, provides the necessary childcare for many mothers to get away from daily routine and cultivate relationships with other women. The bonding and mutual life lessons shared are invaluable.

The program is recommended for the nine-month academic year, however, the summer is necessary for the leadership to meet for planning, staff recruitment, and publicity purposes. The summer also hosts a national homecoming-like gathering for participants of "Coffee Break" ministries across the country.

Convention Press
(Southern Baptist)
127 Ninth Ave. N., Nashville, TN 37234

Children and Missions: Have you ever wondered, "What *is* a Backyard Bible Club?" Occasionally resources materials will refer to material as being "adaptable to a Backyard Bible Club" without explanation of the "club" itself. Convention Press has specifically defined the ministry as an outreach project held in an informal setting such as a backyard, a patio, a carport or garage, a family room or a basement. These clubs reach all children's ages, sometimes collectively. Using Vacation Bible School materials, or similarly prepared materials, the curriculum provides Bible-centered knowledge to children who have little or no knowledge of the Bible and its message. For five days, one and one-half hours per day, a neighborhood can be reached with the gospel message.

Similarly, a Mission VBS is an opportunity to assist families in an area not strong enough to support such a ministry or to establish a new ministry. The schedule is typically two and one-half hours for five days, reaches all age groups (even adults), meets in a building, and requires more staff participants. What a excellent idea for church planting! A minimal investment returns maximum data for beginning a new mission work.

Curriculum is available for both structures.

Foursquare Publications
(Int'l. Church of the Foursquare Gospel)
1910 West Sunset Blvd., Suite 200
Los Angeles, CA 90026

Assimilation and Community Need: What is the church to do about embracing new people for Jesus' sake and protecting our own families from the devastating ills of our society? At a time when all church programs are short staffed, we now must think about the vulnerabilities and legalities of child abuse, malpractice suits, and AIDS infection. These are subjects most are fearful to approach. The Foursquare Church has met the challenge by writing policy statements and others are encouraged to model them or use them as discussion starters for their own approaches. Foursquare ministries are to be commended for their courageous admonition to all churches to become involved because we have the only real source of hope available.

Judson Press
(American Baptist)
P.O. Box 851, Valley Forge, PA 19482

Children's Curriculum: As an alternative to either Vacation Bible School or summer Sunday School, the Vacation Ventures Series, particularly "The Bible: God's Call To Love" is a cooperatively publishing effort of six denominations. Celebrating the Bible is the theme for this kit of lesson materials, music tapes, publicity items, etc. The uniqueness lies in the subject matter. Its contents would enhance any church educational program as children learn to cherish the greatest of all books.

We live in an era of fading absolutes. Children need the underpinning of God's Word and feel confident it is guidebook for their lives. Exploring its pages *can* be fun!

Pathway Press
(Church of God, Cleveland)
1080 Montgomery Ave., Cleveland, TN 37311

Children's Church: Decidedly Pentecostal in style, this publishing house has multiple alternatives for children's worship services. The uniqueness is in the packaging. Everything needed is packaged together: object lessons, puppets, games, skits, and transparencies.

Radiant Life
(Assembly of God)
1445 Boonville Ave., Springfield, MO 65804

Comprehensive Sunday School Curriculum: At a time when many denominations have drastically cut back curriculum publication, this line is in fast forward. Particularly impressive is the "Babies and Toddlers" parenting newsletter, designed to coordinate with the Sunday School ministry.

Randall House Publications
(National Association of Free Will Baptists)
P.O. Box 17306, Nashville, TN 37217

Youth Ministries: Several opportunities are available for Free Will Baptist teens that may inspire cloning. The youth division annually sponsors the denomination's National Youth Conference. Among other activities, young people of all ages participate in two festivals: The National Competitive Activities (Bible memorization and quiz events) and the Music and Arts Festival (competitive musical events in numerous vocal and instrumental categories and dramatic arts; visual arts are also judged competitively). Participants learn the disciplines, and progress through local and state levels before arriving at the national conference.

The Competitive Activities give opportunities for young people to excel using their minds when they may not be physically adept for sports-centered achievement. The Music and Arts Festival provides a opportunity for music and artistic demonstration to be used for the Lord's purposes. So often churches allow these talents to escape to secular outlets.

Much of the staff for the National Conference is provided by two leadership training teams. Outstanding teenagers from across the country, who have demonstrated the fruit of spiritual maturity, are rewarded with entry to this training program (limited to 72 participants). These teens travel to the headquarters, receive intensive training prior the national event, and explore their gifts of leadership during the conference. It is a successful internship providing a solid spiritual basis for personal growth and future ministry opportunities.

Wesley Press
(Free Methodist Church)
8050 Castleway Dr., P.O. Box 50434, Indianapolis, IN 46250

Drop-In Adult Lessons: Published in a series of "How To" articles, these brief topical lessons are compact Scripture, commentary, Bible background information, and Bible dictionary essays in a brief permission-to-photocopy design. The idea of these lessons is to provide a self-contained study in a single lesson; when only one teaching opportunity is available. Not only is it beneficial to the occasional teacher but is an excellent model for novice curriculum designers.

National Association of Free Will Baptists

Open College Campus: Although identified as "Summer Camp," this is not a wilderness experience. Teenagers in grades nine through twelve are invited to the denomination's Bible college campus (Free Will Baptist Bible College, Nashville, TN) to explore vocations and ministry areas available to them through the college.

The program combines a recruitment effort for the college campus and interest channel to the local church youth director. Areas of specialty are *athletic camp, drama camp, missions camp,* and *music camp.* Faculty from the college provide instruction. The importance of the teenager's spiritual life is addressed. Tourist attractions in the area provide recreational breaks. Students meet and are housed on the college campus and become acquainted with its resources and facilities. It is an excellent way to bridge the emphases of several denominational departments.

For Further Discussion

1. Define evangelicalism. According to this definition, is your church "evangelical"? Why or why not?
2. What is a parachurch organization and what are some of its purposes?
3. What are some examples of parachurch organizations in your local area?
4. What is a scriptural basis for the unity of all believers?
5. What are some activities in your local area which seek to bring believers together in a demonstration of their spiritual unity?

For Application

1. If your church is a member of a denomination or fellowship, what unique ministries do they provide or encourage in the summer months?
2. Call a local church in your area who is not a member of your own fellowship or denomination. Ask to speak to the senior pastor or minister of Christian education. Inquire regarding the summer ministry programs which are provided by that particular group.
3. What are some concrete ways your church can display its spiritual unity with other Bible-believing churches in your community?

Other Denominational Publishing Houses

Abingdon Press (United Methodist)
201 Eighth Ave. S., Nashville, TN 37202

Augsburg Fortress (American Lutheran Church)
426 S. Fifth St. Box 1209, Minneapolis, MN 55440

Christian Board of Publications (a.k.a. Cooperative Publishing Assn. supported by Christian Church, Church of the Brethren, Cumberland Presbyterian, Friends General Conference, Friends United, Moravian Church, United Church of Christ)
Box 179, St. Louis, MO 63166

Concordia Publishing House (Lutheran Church, Missouri Synod)
3558 South Jefferson Ave., St. Louis, MO 63118

Faith & Fellowship Press (Church of the Lutheran Brethren)
704 W. Vernon Ave., Fergus Falls, MN 56538-0655

Faith & Life Press (General Conference Mennonites)
P.O. Box 347, Newton, KS 67114-0347

Pentecostal Publishing House (United Pentecostal Church)
8855 Dunn Road, Hazelwood, MO 53042

Regular Baptist Press (Regular Baptist)
1300 N. Meachum Road, Schaumburg, IL 60173

LOCAL CHURCH INSPIRED PROGRAMS

9

First and Second Timothy have much to say about the care and progress of the local church. The local church has a responsibility to care for the needs of all its members. Viewing the local church as a family can provide much inspiration for new ministry opportunities; many of which can be addressed during the summer months.

The sixth chapter of 1 Timothy acknowledges there is much about living and working together daily which could produce strife. Yet we are encouraged to examine our attitudes toward one another in light of the nurturing work of the local church. As we uphold one another, caring for the needs of the body, we demonstrate the caring nature of God to the community around us. As a family, we want to address our members' needs to keep the family healthy and happy.

Many local congregations allow their loving concern for one another to activate their imaginations for the glory of God. Following are examples of programs which were born and grew when the needs of a local church were met by the surrendered gifts of one or more members willing to organize a structure *not* available from the church marketplace. Some of these programs have won such favor that they are, at this printing, being prepared for publication. Others are still shared through correspondence requests. To spare many church clerical workers the time and expense of detailed information, the *Instructor's Guide* for this text provides organizational frameworks for beginning a similar effort in your church.

Inter-generational Programs

The whole family can get involved, one way or another, with the following efforts.

Ministry Fair (Recruitment)

As one church year closes and another begins, there are numerous volunteer positions to fill. As a church grows, so do the opportunities for service. The Ministry Fair provides an "exhibit" approach designed to familiarize old and new members with programs and ministries of the church. A large area (fellowship hall, gymnasium, lawn) is subdivided into "booth space" such as you would encounter at a county fair or convention exhibit hall. A 10-foot by 10-foot booth nicely accommodates most church tables; however smaller spaces are workable. One booth should be assigned for every ministry supported by volunteer service and finances. All the Christian education programs, music ministry programs, mission agencies or missionaries you support, can be represented with their own booth. Even committees seeking volunteer members can prepare a booth. Current volunteers from the ministry are responsible for depicting the emphasis of their ministry or to display literature used in the function of that ministry. Staff the booths with a representative (rotating representatives if the exhibit time will be long) who can sign up interested individuals. Each ministry will then have a list of persons to contact about suitability for service, rather than the "cold call" approach many churches still use.

Summer In The Park (Community and Fellowship)

As a change of pace for inviting friends and families who otherwise will not accompany you to the church property, a summer church service slot (most often an evening service) is relocated to an area park. The openness of the setting alone mandates an invitation for the community to "come and join" the activities. A concert, drama, or notable personality draws people to the area. The activity carries an evangelistic witness. There is no pressure for visitors to identify themselves other than in friendly greetings to people nearby. The event *is* openly sponsored by the church so these visitors will know where to come should they desire more assistance.

Sunday Nights Of Summer (Concert Series)

Christian music enthusiasts enjoy a concert series, particularly when a variety of musical styles and artists are offered. The series patterns many community models which offer secular music artists. It may be scheduled as an outdoor event, similar to the "Summer In The Park" idea above or held indoors, using a facility appropriate for the music involved. The basic outreach idea is to provide an open door for friends and family to invite persons curious about the church family, yet not ready to become involved in regular programming. A reception, with simple refreshments, may follow the concert, providing opportunity to meet the artists and other concert attenders. Share the work by rotating reception duties among several groups within the church.

Summerfest (Special Interest Classes with an outreach purpose)

"Summerfest" is a great way to maintain the interest of adults whose commitment may wane in the summer months as well as to attract new adults in your community to the church. "Summerfest" is designed around topics of general interest which are practical, not specifically biblical, in scope. There is a wide range of potential topics. Good choices for topics can be shared hobbies or "how to" interests.

A "Summerfest" committee should be appointed to determine what topics to offer, how many sessions, who will be the leaders, and when the sessions will be offered. You may choose to run the program over a weekend, for adults only, or make it a week-long approach that runs simultaneously with a children's VBS.

Guest instructors, from the church or community, are invited to demonstrate a skill (such as calligraphy or gourmet cooking), inform about a topic (such as auto tune-up or investments), or to lead a discussion of pooled knowledge (such as tips on gardening or buying antiques). Whatever suits the cultural interest of the local church and the people who interface in daily life is the common ground for selecting the interest classes. It is best if several classes can be going on at the same time, so as to attract a wider audience and keep the class sizes down to a small number for better interaction. Choose times (evening hours and weekends) when the majority of working people will be able to attend.

The best "Summerfests" will offer the interest classes for one hour, followed immediately by an invitation to join a large gathering for enjoying a "guest" lecturer or notable personality who shares from his or her personal (or professional) life; giving emphasis to the application of God's direction in that life.

Some "Summerfest" programs conclude with a family night or family fair when everyone can enjoy the good company of one another and model wholesome recreation.

Interest Area Ministries

Some local churches have developed a summer tradition of offering ministry opportunities which they are unable to present throughout the year. These ideas take on a more direct spiritual purpose.

Featured Asset

The Hawthorne Gospel Church in New Jersey offers a summer-long "Bible Conference" incorporating nationally-known Bible teachers, evangelists, and musicians. By spanning the entire summer, it is difficult *not* to find an opportunity to schedule participation in the conference or be unable to bring a friend. This large church intentionally schedules its bookstore and lending library to be open for the conference attenders. The church has identified its greatest asset, then ambitiously and aggressively offered it to the community at large.

Libraries

Libraries themselves offer interesting avenues for several different spiritual gifts. Local schools and public library book clubs (or reading programs) give inspiration for similar ventures by the church. Using many different names, all these programs identify Christian book "reading clubs" and children's "story hours." Persons with administrative skills oversee the scheduling of facilities and inventory. Others with communication skills can publicize the events and featured books. Storytellers share inspirational thrillers from the lives of missionaries or well-prepared children's fiction. Older church members enjoy the suggested reading lists as they take recommended titles along on their vacation trips. The libraries also sponsor travel information or travel presentations when overseas trips prove particularly interesting.

Group-specific Inspiration

Most local members have a special burden for the area of ministry where they serve. Highly committed workers will eventually identify an unmet need. Existing programs, curriculum publications, and the search for a workshop or seminar, to provide assistance, may not be available. Such has been the circumstances for the Lord to create a most unique opportunity.

Greenhouse (A Shared Common Meal)

The old-fashioned church supper has been given a facelift and offered whenever the church family can share a meal *together*. Most often this will be a mid-week gathering, perhaps prior to another popular scheduled event. In other churches it may follow the Sunday service. Whatever time is chosen, the sharing of a meal nurtures and bonds the community the way gathering around the table reinforces family life at home. Much like the sharing of loaves and fishes in Matthew 14, which provided Jesus the object lesson to illustrate the impact of a community surrendered to God, so these meals provide an opportunity for fellowship within the church as well as outreach into the community.

G.R.I.T.S. (Gettin' Right In The Summer)

A youth program designed for the collective purpose of companionship, worship, and teaching teens of all ages. Many small churches do not have sufficient staff to spin off young teens from older teens or college-age singles. Larger churches find the summer months equally challenging as volunteers are not available for regular programming. Setting aside time, purposely, for the experience of older teens to influence the younger ones is valuable for everyone; not just a means to compensate for the lack of adult leadership.

Heart To Heart (Women helping women)

This program is not necessarily a partnership between older women and younger women, but of the spiritually mature with women younger in the faith. The program begins with a survey approach of interested parties. Each woman identifies herself as a senior or junior volunteer, as described above. A small committee, representing female leadership personnel, reviews the responses and makes suggestions of who might be a helpful "friend" to whom. The two, or three, parties have agreed at sign-up time to give the relationship an honest effort to flourish (usually a designated period of time is determined, perhaps a year) and meetings are arranged independently thereafter. First meetings are usually an invitation from the senior partner to tea, or whatever is comfortable to her. As the friendship grows, natural opportunities develop to get together. A valuable prayer partner, trusted Christian friend, and adviser is the intended goal. At the end of the designated time, it is understood, regular meetings may or may not continue; depending upon what has transpired in those lives. Sometimes, in these busy days, friendships need an impetus to grow and this program may provide such.

Man To Man (Male role modeling)

Similar to the above program, men more often than women need the discipline of scheduling time with a prayer partner or role model who will give advice from a biblical perspective. The details for matching individuals may be tedious; however, what price can be placed on friendship?

Network Serving Seminars (Spiritual Gifts Analysis)

A valuable tool for volunteer recruitment efforts is to knowledge-ably place persons where they are most likely to succeed. This program, born through the Willow Creek Church (Barrington, IL) by creator Bruce Bugbee, is now being offered for wider distribution through Zondervan Publishing. The basic concept is to assist Christians in idenitfying their spiritual gifts and to begin exercising them in the context of the local church. The seminar format, of multiple sessions, guides participants through key areas via simple "testing" vehicles and group Bible discovery. At each session a different facet is explored; such as Servanthood (through personal trait and observation assessments), Scripture (through experience and conviction assessments), Stewardship (through support gift, temperament, and ministry assessments) and a Servant Profile. All the spiritual gifts are defined by numerous scripture references. The "assessments" (testing) are not right versus wrong responses; rather identification of the participant's passions, temperaments, talents, maturity, etc. The program is an interesting approach to a timeless need.

S.I.C.M. (Summer Institute for Children's Ministry)

Verbally referenced as "sick 'em," this program communicates an assertive approach to dealing with idle children during the summer months. Many urban and suburban settings are demanding more participation from churches. Typically, church doors are kept locked during summer midweek days, even though neighborhood children may be wandering the neighborhood looking for activity. This program is great for a summer internship if you have college-age or young adults looking for ministry experience.

A coordinator should be secured early in the spring to organize the events. Four to six weeks would be best to arrange a variety of options. Each week would feature a different activity. A typical week of summer camp, at a resident facility, may be included. However, much of the selected activities are to be done within the neighborhood of the church. One week may feature a popular sports "camp" (like soccer or basketball) where kids receive instruction in sharpening their skills and learning about God's team at the same time. Area facilities will dictate the sport. A week of Backyard Bible Clubs can blitz the town with small groups designed to reach just one street or city block. Another week may be a "B.A.C.K." Day Camp (Breakaway Adventure Camp for Kids), where the church lawn or area park is used as the camp site. Kids bring a sack lunch and spend the day doing skits, crafts, scavenger hunts, and Bible lessons. Only the imagination limits the options for your church's S.I.C.M.

S.T.A.M.P. (Short-Term Adult Mission Program)

What better way to rally support for missions than to sponsor adults willing to spend this year's vacation on a mission field in active service. Each church must decide how they will fund the operation (see the *Instructor's Guide* for suggestions), but the skills and spiritual gifts of your lay people can be incorporated into active missionary service on a short-term basis. Denominational mission boards and some inter-denominational agencies may be able to use the skills you have to offer. Trade skills (construction, engineering) are particularly valuable. Teachers are often needed to tutor English language skills and doctors or nurses can provide welcome relief to understaffed clinics. It is best to contact a missions agency or a specific missionary your church supports before determining to go overseas. If foreign travel is an obstacle, there are many areas within your own country where people are in need and God's blessing for missionary service can be just as fulfilling.

Ultimate Issues (Visitor Assimilation)

This ministry grew from a short-term experiment into a year-round feature at one local church. Begin by identifying the most-asked questions, or areas of curiosity, from unchurched friends and relatives. Next identify a person, or panel, who could speak to the subject or answer questions and be a fine testimony of God's working in the lives of ordinary people. Assign the topic and week it is to be addressed. The topics could range from curiosities about the Bible to contemporary issues in the news, or current events in the community. Visitors to your church are invited to this one-week presentation when they are uncomfortable about joining an established group or simply interested in investigating Christianity. The setting should be as non-threatening as possible. Speakers should avoid religious cliches. This is an excellent way to introduce newcomers to the caring, thoughtful church family.

Summary

Has an interesting idea for creative ministry crossed your mind? Would your church be willing to examine the needs of its members and determine what ministry approach is missing during the summer months? Perhaps there is a creative approach to the problem. Even a one-time commitment to try something new could bring a neighbor to the Lord who would not have otherwise felt comfortable to approach the church. Members within the local church can also find new relationships and meaningful ministry during the summer when they take time to become reacquainted with the church family.

For Further Discussion

1. What are the various ministries of your church which would be involved in a "Ministry Fair"?
2. What are the advantages and/or disadvantages of having special services during the summer months somewhere other than your church's facilities?
3. What are some additional summer ministry ideas for children, youth, women, and men?

For Application

1. Come up with your own list of "Summerfest" topics that would be attractive to the non-churched in your community.
2. Check with the mission organizations (both home and foreign) which are supported by your church. Ask them specifically for information about short-term mission opportunities for youth and adults.
3. If money, time, and resources were unlimited, list the S.I.C.M. activities you believe would minister effectively to the children in your church and community.
4. Imagine that your church is starting an "Ultimate Issues" class. What topics would you want to cover and who in your congregation would lead each topic?

Organizations Which Can Help

Campus Crusade For Christ Int'l.
New Life Resources
304 Dividend Drive
Peachtree City, GA 30269

D.C. Cook's Nursery Time
850 N. Grove Avenue
Elgin, IL 60120

Global Advance
Hands-On Missions
P.O. Box 222
Rockwall, TX 75087

Mobile Missionary Assistance
 Program
1736 N. Sierra Bonita
Pasadena, CA 91104
818-791-8663

Shepherd Ministries
2845 West Airport Freeway
Suite 137
Irving, TX 75062

Summer Bible Conference
The Hawthorne Gospel Church
Route 208
Hawthorne, NJ 07506

The Church Library Handbook
Harvest House Publishers
1075 Arrowsmith
Eugene, OR 97402

The Zondervan Corporation
5300 Patterson S.E.
Grand Rapids, MI 49530

CREATIVE CAMPING

10

What comes to your mind when you hear the word "camping"? It may be a picture of carrying a backpack along a trail and later struggling to pitch an overnight tent. It may be a memory of living with a group of 6 kids in a cramped cabin, under the direction of a not-much-older counselor, and going together to an archery range or craft class. You may remember long hikes in the woods, rappelling up a mountain cliff, rafting down a gurgling river, or sitting around a campfire singing songs and telling stories. For some of you, the word "camping" means a time and a place when you decided to give your life totally to God. Today, camping can be all of these images—and more!

The most basic definition of camping is "outdoor living." The American Camping Association's definition is a bit more detailed, "a sustained experience in group living in a natural environment under the supervision of trained leaders." To define Christian camping, you need only to add the word "Christian" between "group" and "living" and you've got a general idea of what camping is about. However, an even better way of describing Christian camping, especially creative Christian camping, is to understand it as an activity which seeks to utilize full-day learning experiences, held in various settings, as an opportunity for discipling individuals toward maturity in Jesus Christ. Thus, Christian camping is, above all else, camping with a purpose!

How Did Camping Originate?

The roots of modern-day Christian camping go back to the "camp meetings" of the 19th century. These meetings were times when whole families would gather at a central location for times of preaching, teaching, singing, and of course, fellowship. Although the programming was designed primarily for adults, these camp meetings were in many ways precursors to today's family camps.

Fredrick William Gunn holds the distinction as the father of the American camping movement. Gunn organized his first camp for boys in 1861. It was 1880 when George Hinckley, a pastor in Connecticut, directed the first church-sponsored resident camp in the United States. Five years later, the YMCA held their first camp and in 1907 the Boy Scouts got in on the act.

The camping movement exploded in the 1900s, growing from 2,000 resident camps in 1920 to over 6,000 in 1950 to over 12,000 today (both secular and Christian). For many young people in America, summer means they will have a camping experience of some kind, an experience which most of them will look forward to passionately. Check out your local newspaper during the spring months and you will likely discover advertisements for all types of camping experiences.

Two Broad Categories of Camping

Camping can be either unstructured or structured. *Unstructured* camping is what happens when a group of your friends at church decide to go on an overnight camping trip to a local state park. You divide up the responsibilities, agree to meet at a certain time and place, and then enjoy being with each other for 24 to 36 hours. Although this is certainly camping in the broad sense, this is not what we mean when we discuss utilizing creative camping as vital ministry of your church in the summer months. *Structured* camping simply means that the camping experience is carefully planned by those who have experience and training in the field. The structured camping experience has a focused purpose relating to helping those involved progress in their spiritual maturity. This chapter will cover the various aspects of a structured, organized approach to Christian camping.

Values of the Camping Experience

Why is camping such an effective tool for Christian education? Its effectiveness is in part due to the elements valued in a creative camping program.

Completely Different Setting

One of the key distinctives of camping is that it is done in a natural environment. While this setting could be the church's backyard, more than likely it will be in a location either partially different or totally different than that experienced in the normal day-to-day life of the campers. This difference is more than mere novelty. Often, the change of pace and the new sights, sounds, smells, and sensations of the camp setting help to create an atmosphere where campers are more open to what God is doing in the world and what God wants to accomplish in their lives.

Compressed Time

Although the clock runs at the same speed at camp as it does at home, there is great value in the fact that everyone does not go home at the end of the 11 o'clock service to eat lunch and watch a sports contest on TV. In a camping experience the clock takes on a entirely new meaning. Instead of one hour of Sunday School teaching interrupted by 168 hours until the next Sunday, one hour of solid Bible instruction is followed by living with the same group for 12 hours until it is time for some more Bible instruction. In a normal environment, students have every distraction and reason to forget what was learned 168 hours ago, but in camping, every lesson is followed by real life where the lesson can be digested, applied, argued, discussed and, hopefully, used by God to transform the lives of campers. Many would argue that one week in a Christian camping experience (96 to 144 hours) can accomplish more than a year in a Sunday School class (40 to 50 hours).

Controlled Atmosphere

People often complain about the "rat race" of life and the seemingly endless events which crowd their lives. Another value of a camping experience is that it breaks out of the routine in such a way that things which can often distract from spiritual growth are not in the way. In most camping experiences, for example, television is strictly prohibited (unless there is a particular video to be watched by the group), as well as personal tape players and radios. In fact, some camps do not even provide a daily newspaper. Many adults look forward to being in a place where only emergency phone calls are allowed.

The atmosphere at camp, however, is more than just different. If properly conducted, every aspect of the camping experience is designed to further the goal of stimulating Christian maturity. Yes, camp is designed to be a controlled environment. But it is controlled with a purpose and, thus, is usually viewed by the participants as refreshing instead of confining.

Close-Up View of Life

It has often been said, "Christianity is more caught than taught." Christian camping provides an opportunity for discovering that Christianity is more than a belief system, it is a way of life. It is one thing to hear someone teach a truth on Sunday morning. It is another to see that person live that truth on Monday afternoon during a highly competitive game of softball. This aspect of a camping experience can be especially meaningful for the person who has not enjoyed the blessing of being raised in a Christian home. Camping allows Christian leaders to demonstrate that their faith really works in everyday situations.

This value of camping is one of the reasons it is important to utilize leaders who are gifted and trained in camping ministry.

Someone else has said, "What you are speaks so loudly that I cannot hear what you are saying." If you choose the wrong people to lead a camping experience, it can have long-term negative effects.

Relationship Building

Camping is the stuff of life. This is why it is such a powerful educational tool. In camping, campers are not just learning together—they are living together. Campers are often forced to communicate with other people even if they do not want to. Camping demands interaction with others for prolonged periods of time. As campers are confronted with truths from God's Word, relationships will often become the focus. Campers will be challenged to establish or renew a relationship with God as well as to develop strong relationships with others both inside and outside the body of Christ.

Personal Insight

Many young people and adults do not have a clear understanding of who they are in the sight of God. For some, it is because they have been brought up in an unwholesome family situation. For others, it is because they have never had clear teaching from God's Word on the subject. For still others, they have been intimidated by peer pressure. Part of a solid camping program will seek to develop a biblical view of personhood. This can be accomplished not just by teaching on the subject, but primarily in providing opportunities of personal challenge as well as one-on-one counseling.

Skill/Spiritual Gift Development

A camp program should include many new, or at least different, experiences. Campers should be given opportunities to develop new skills or improve the ones they already have. Many of these skills will be related to the physical distinctives of the camp property. For example, at a facility with a waterfront, opportunities should be given for canoeing, waterskiing, scuba diving, and water safety/lifeguard training. If a camp has access to hills or mountains with cliffs, rock climbing may be its specialty. As campers gain skills in new areas, other things, such as a renewed level of self-confidence, will emerge.

In addition to teaching skills relating to the camp property, young people and adults should be challenged to discern and develop their spiritual gifts. In the camping context, many opportunities for "trying out" possible spiritual gifts can be available. For example, a young woman who thinks she may have the gift of teaching may be given an opportunity to lead a small group Bible study. A young man who believes he may have the gift of encouragement might be assigned to work with someone with low self-esteem on a project. Camp is a great place to do more than just talk about spiritual gifts—opportunities should abound to live them!

Biblical View of the Environment

Camping programs should seek to utilize the outdoors as much as possible. For many Americans, the majority of life is spent indoors. Many do not know the names of trees, wildflowers, and other plants. Many cannot name stars and constellations. Others do not know the wildlife in a particular location, their traits and practices. In addition to learning more about the world of nature, the camp experience can be a great setting to study what God's Word says about the environment and what the Christian's attitude and responsibility should be toward it.

Leadership Development

If you want to discover who the real leaders are in a group of young people or adults, place them in a camping experience. Usually, observation alone will reveal who the leaders are as well as those with leadership potential. Camping provides many opportunities to exercise leadership as well as to learn leadership. CIT programs (Counselor In Training) provide opportunities for older high school and college students to "work their way through the ranks" at a Christian camp. Other camping programs are designed specifically to help young people and/or adults develop the leadership skills they need to make an impact on their world for Christ.

Types of Camping Experiences

The number of different camping programs has greatly expanded in the past twenty years. Today, camping experiences are limited only by your imagination and budget. Many churches utilize the programs and facilities of camps which are either independently-owned or owned by a district, state, or national denominational board. Some larger churches may own their own camp facilities. Yet others will rent camp facilities while providing the program staff themselves. Exactly how you do it will be dependent on the resources available to you in your particular situation.

Day Camps

Day camps are, as the name implies, programmed for the daylight hours only. This type of camping has gained in popularity because it can be done almost anywhere at a fraction of the cost of a regular resident camp. The current facilities of a church or Christian school can be easily adapted for this type of camp program. A church bus or several vans can put the campers in touch with local parks, forest preserves, and other nature sites. While a day camp should not be VBS with a name change, VBS curriculum can often by used as the Bible study and craft portion of the program. However, day camp programs should seek to emulate resident camps as much as possible.

One of the advantages of day camping is that children too young for overnight camping programs can be involved. Even preschoolers can enjoy and benefit from a well-designed day camp experience.

Resident Camps

Resident camps involve an overnight stay varying from one night to a week or more. Resident camping is the total camp experience. While certainly more expensive than a day camp program, the returns will often be greater as well. There are several options you can consider ranging from owning and developing your own site to renting a full-service facility.

If you rent, you can decide the level of programs and services provided by the camp itself. In some cases, you may provide all personnel, from counselors and cooks to recreation leaders and teaching staff. In other cases, the camp may provide food service, counselors and recreation staff while you provide the campers and the teaching staff. And there are all levels of options in between the two extremes. Of course, there are camps available which provide everything except the campers. All you do is show up and they do the rest (see the section *Where to Find Camping Resources*).

Specialty Camps

Specialty camps will include the spiritual emphasis of other camping approaches but will build recreation time around a particular sport or other special emphasis. In recent years, sports camps of all kinds have flourished. If your children play a certain sport, you can usually find a Christian camp which can provide a program specifically for that sport. Football camps, basketball camps, soccer camps, and baseball camps are just a few options available.

A number of camp programs are beginning to emphasize various forms of the arts. There are music camps (for both instrumentalists and vocalists), art camps (painting, sculpture, etc.) and drama camps to name a few.

Wilderness Camping

Wilderness camping is camping at its basic essentials. As the name implies, this is life out of a backpack. This approach usually involves a small group of 8 to 10 who are accompanied by a trained guide/counselor. The campers cook their own meals, set-up and tear-down their own campsites, and spend the entire time in the outdoors. The trained guide/counselor will seek to guide the participants through a camping experience which will stretch them mentally, physically, and spiritually. While not designed for young children, this type of camping is often well accepted by teenagers and young adults. A word of warning: make sure you utilize a trained professional as your guide/counselor. This type of camping experience is definitely not for a novice leader. The results could be disastrous.

Bike Trip Camping

As bike riding has grown in popularity among the general population, so has the development of bike trip camping. Bike trips require the leadership of an experienced leader. This approach is similar to wilderness camping except each person rides a bicycle. Obviously, a bike trip will be limited to paved roads or smooth off-road trails. Since bike trips can cover a lot of miles in a day (from 15 to 30 miles), a great deal of advance planning has to be made, especially in reserving camp sites for each night. Some churches may combine a bike trip with another project such as riding to a church in a rural area where a 5-day club or VBS program is conducted before riding home at the end of the week. Warning: be sure the participants are experienced bikers and physically prepared for the distance you want to travel to avoid potential problems. Often, bike trips will go much better if there is a support van or pick-up truck which can haul all of the gear for the trip (food, tents, sleeping bags, etc.) as well as be available for emergencies.

Rafting Trip Camping

Rafting trip camping is similar to wilderness camping and bike trip camping except you are traveling by canoe. As with any camping of this type, an experienced leader and careful advance planning is an absolute necessity.

Family Camping

Many churches are discovering the positive benefits of a week at a camp or conference center for entire families, instead of just one age group. Usually, one church or a small group of churches, will plan a week at camp for the whole family to attend together. The schedule is similar to a "regular" resident camp with the exception of activities purposely designed to bring age groups together instead of separating them. The benefits of such an approach are not limited to what happens during the week at camp but will usually have a profound carryover into the life of the church during the rest of the year.

A unique type of family camping occurs when families who own or rent recreational vehicles (R.V.s) decide to travel in caravan fashion. The program may be designed to travel to a particular site where the R.V.s will be parked for several days or a route may be planned where the R.V.s park at a different site each night.

Special Emphasis Camping
There is almost no limit to the varieties of camping programs available to the local church who is committed to being creative in its approach. Any age group, or any group with a special need or common characteristic, can be the basis for a camp program. Camp programs can be designed for single adults, married couples, senior adults, divorced adults, single parents (with or without children; the children may be attending their own week at camp), the church staff, the Sunday School teachers and Christian education workers, the church choir, and so on. Camping is an activity that cuts across age lines and interest areas.

Where to Find Camp Resources

One of the best sources of information about Christian camps and conference centers is Christian Camping International/USA (CCI/USA). CCI/USA has 750 member camps and conference centers in the United States and many more that are located overseas. CCI/USA provides a service called the *Christian Camp and Conference Center GUIDEPAK*. The *GUIDEPAK* contains complete information about CCI/USA member camps and is available on both a regional and national basis. The address and phone number of CCI/USA is given at the end of this chapter.

CCI/USA also publishes the *Journal of Christian Camping* (5 issues a year) which deals exclusively with issues relating to Christian camping. CCI/USA produces many additional resources for those involved in various camping ministries.

Another source of information on Christian camping is available from the two leading non-denominational club programs for churches, Pioneer Clubs and Awana Clubs. Both organizations direct a ministry of camping through their own facilities and have camping programs in the United States and Canada. Keep in mind that in order to participate in the camping program of Pioneer Clubs or Awana Clubs, your church must be active in that particular program. Write or call them for the information you desire.

Many denominations also direct camping programs on the district, state, and national level. Contact the Christian education department of your denomination to learn more about what camping options are provided.

Summary

Christian camping programs and summer time just naturally go together. Creative Christian camping is an activity which seeks to utilize full-day learning experiences, held in various settings, as an opportunity for discipling individuals toward maturity in Jesus Christ.

Although camping had its origins in the "camp meetings" of the 1800s, it began to flourish in the early 1900s and today has grown to thousands of camps and conference centers within reach of almost every community in America. Camping can be either unstructured or structured. The structured camping experience is designed to help its participants progress toward spiritual maturity.

A creative camping program is based on several values which contribute to its overall goal. Everything in the camping experience is designed to enhance every aspect of the camper's life. The values of a completely different setting, the compressed time factor, a controlled atmosphere, a close-up view of life, an emphasis on relationship building and personal insight, the development of skills and spiritual gifts, a biblical view of the environment, and leadership development, all combine to help produce a well-rounded, spiritually-maturing Christian.

Camp programs can be either day camp only or residential in scope. There are many different types of camps: specialty camps, wilderness camping, bike trip camping, raft trip camping, family camping, and special interest camping; all are possibilities for creative summer ministry.

CCI/USA can provide you with information on camp and conference facilities. Pioneer Clubs and Awana Clubs both run camping programs for their constituencies. Often, your own denomination will provide resources in the area of camping.

Opportunities abound for the churches who are willing to make the commitment to creative camping in their summer ministries program.

For Further Discussion

1. How did organized camping begin in the United States?
2. What is the difference between the two major types of camping?
3. In your opinion, what are the two most important values of Christian camping and why?
4. What is a CIT program?
5. What do you think are the advantages and disadvantages of renting camp facilities instead of owning them?
6. What are the values of a wilderness camp program?
7. Is a wilderness camping program for everybody? Why or why not?

For Application

1. What camping facilities have been used by your church in recent months?
2. If your church is a member of a denomination, fellowship, or network, have someone in the class write or call for information on their camping ministry.
3. Call up several of the Christian camps in your area and ask for additional information (brochures, camp schedules, etc.) on the camp.

4. What types of camping programs have been done in your church over the past 2 or 3 years? What camping programs would you like to see developed in your church and why?
5. Select one type of camp program. Design a daily schedule which would contain all of the major elements of the program.

Organizations Which Can Help

American Camping Association
Bradford Woods
Martinsville, IN 46151
317-342-8456

Pioneer Clubs/Camp Cherith
Box 788
Wheaton, IL 60189
708-293-1600

Awana Clubs International
One East Bode Rd.
Streamwood, IL 60103
708-213-2000

Pioneer Clubs Canada, Inc.
Camp Cherith
Box 5447
Burlington, ON L7R 4L2
416-681-2883

Christian Camping International
P.O. Box 62189
Colorado Springs, CO 80962
719-260-9400

SUMMER MINISTRY & COMMUNITY NEED

11

How intentional are your summer ministry plans? Raleigh Washington and Glen Kehrein write, in the July/August 1993 issue of *Moody Magazine*, how we as Christians live, work, and even worship side-by-side with diverse members of our society, yet remain alienated from one another. Without an intentional effort to shed preconceived ideas about one another, there can be no flow of ministry. Washington and Kehrein are particularly concerned about relationships crossing racial barriers. Jesus was also concerned about relationships crossing social, economic, racial, and emotional barriers. Much of His time was spent with the poor, the sick, and the hurting.

Even in Jesus' day, His followers were so occupied with the details of ministry, they often failed to see the needs immediately around them. Matthew 15:23 records the thoughtless response of the disciples to an annoying woman who persisted in making a lot of noise. She belonged to another culture, easy to disregard as an outcast. Yet Jesus rewarded her simple faith and healed her daughter from demon possession.

Romans 15:1-2 records this instruction, "Now we who are strong ought to bear the weaknesses of those without strength and not just please ourselves. Let each of us please his neighbor for his good, to his edification." Servanthood begins with a careful look at the people close at hand. A fresh look at community need begins within your church, on your street, and in your town. Even the simple cup of water given in the Lord's name will demonstrate obedience and glorify God.

The Poor

Challenging economic times present dilemmas for the most carefully monitored family budgets. Neighbors helping neighbors is a concept in decline as crime and fear grip a community. Some towns may have noticeably visible economic lines while others will not be so prominent. Consider what you or your church might do to meet the basic necessities of life for whomever may need assistance.

Homelessness is rapidly rising. Churches will need to be more open and cooperative with civic services for the homeless. If there is no referral network in your town, consider beginning one with other nearby churches. Gather for discussion with leaders who can sort out the available facilities and goods, as well as create rotating schedules for everyone to share in the responsibility. The homeless are in need of all kinds of community services reserved for *residents*—tutors for children, library and recreation facilities, and transportation (if no public system is available).

If a shelter or rescue mission is already operating in your community, consider volunteering time to serve food, do laundry, or perform other necessary services. Are you a retail merchant with goods that could be donated to such a facility?

Resale shops and yard sales are popular. Consider sponsoring one or the other as a ministry of the church. The self-esteem of the purchaser will remain intact as the dollars stretch the purchasing power.

Illiteracy is at crisis proportions. People of all ages are dysfunctional with its crippling effects. Consider offering your services to a tutoring agency or, if you are a qualified teacher, begin your own service.

What community is not touched by immigration? Assimilating into a new community is difficult for anyone. If you were to relocate to another country, many everyday assumptions would need to be reexamined. Perhaps you could be the friend someone needs with a welcoming service. If a large ethnic population exists in your town, consider beginning a more specific outreach to that group.

You may find you do not have to go far to literally impact the world for Jesus Christ. In one community, a local junior college has over 1500 foreign students from over 25 different countries. Away from home and in a foreign culture, these students are often open to the warm embrace of people who genuinely care about them.

The Sick

Illness does not take a vacation. The medically dependent and disabled can feel more deserted during the summer months than any other time of year. There are no holiday traditions to tug at the heartstrings of the healthy and more fortunate. Consider volunteer assistance for someone who would appreciate being wheeled outdoors, escorted on a walk, or taken shopping. Perhaps someone needs a ramp built or a helping hand with rehabilitative exercises. Perhaps you could help organize a blood drive through the Red Cross or local hospital referral. Who is on the church prayer list and can you be the answer to their prayers?

If you are a medical professional, there may be a volunteer service looking for your skills. Dentists can become missionaries. Numerous outdoor events, sponsored by area churches, will need first aid attendants. What activities are taking place around you where your expertise could be selflessly contributed?

Catastrophic illnesses leave many in its wake. A ministry of prayer and encouragement can be shared with the families and care-givers who tend to persons stricken with dreaded diseases.

The Hurting

Pain comes in many forms. Some pain is a result of sin and poor choices within our own lives. Other pain can result from the sin of others who share the world with us. In other cases pain is simply a result of living in a fallen world.

The widowed mate needs care. The mourning process is often slow and agonizing. If death has taken a spouse suddenly, the preparations for living alone may not be in order. The New Testament church modeled for us the careful attention we should be giving to the needs of the bereaved. Is there more we can do when the burial is completed and life continues on?

Coping with the end result of someone's desperate deed abruptly introduces some people to the arena of prison ministry. Our prison population has increased 150% in the last decade. It may surprise you to know prisons need volunteers, also. The accelerated demand for stopping crime has left criminal justice systems short on funds, equipment, repair and construction services. An excellent test of your servant attitude would be to approach a prison chaplain with a blank sheet of paper and allow him to fill in the need.

Hurting people are all around us who have been betrayed, rejected, or feel unwanted. Divorce, crisis pregnancy, acts of violence, child neglect, joblessness, suicide, to name a few, dominate our news headlines. Any one of these points could provide entry for a Christian witness if you care enough to tackle the issue.

Something as simple as hospitality can open more than homes; hearts can be opened to the life-changing power of the Lord. Christmas Coffees are an informal way to open your home to neighbors so they can see firsthand the meaning of Christmas as it effects the life of your family. Organization and promotion for these social gatherings begins early in the summer. The summer barbecue grill, a bowl of homemade ice cream, or cool beverage might provide the same opportunity to share a word of testimony with your neighbors. "Do not neglect to show hospitality to strangers, for by this some have entertained angels without knowing it" (Heb. 13:2).

Others Around You

It is not only the impoverished who need to feel the hand of God. The successful and explosive ministry of Willow Creek Church began with Bill Hybels and others who acknowledged a burden for the unique needs of a specific community, a segment of society. Today, they give leadership to an international network of churches ministering to the unchurched.

A recent Christian magazine profiled the ministry of former school teacher and Korean missionary, Tillie Burgin. After Tillie and her husband returned from the mission field, due to illness, she was put to work by her church as minister of home missions. From a tentative start in 1986, Tillie's effort at reaching the needy of Arlington, Texas, has grown from a one-woman operation to a ministry of over 600 volunteers. Today, Tillie heads up Mission Arlington, a ministry which provides food, clothing, medical care, and the gospel of Jesus Christ to those who have been neglected and often forgotten. This effective ministry started with the faithful efforts of one woman, who was determined to make a difference in her community with God's help.

Wayne Gordon, a young white man, moved to Lawndale, a predominantly black neighborhood on the southwest side of Chicago in 1975. Supporting himself as an assistant football coach at a local public school, he started a youth ministry with several team members. From that group grew Lawndale Community Church, a 500-member interracial congregation. Today, the church sponsors a medical clinic, a tutoring program, a thrift shop, and a building renovation ministry that has remodeled scores of community apartments. Lawndale Church is currently lead by a black pastor, Carey Casey, while Gordon is in charge of community outreach for the church. The strong working relationship and friendship demonstrated by this interracial leadership team is having a positive effect on all of the ministries of the church.

Summary

It will be *your* insightful obedience which God uses to reach *your* community. Following the example of Jesus to embrace those nearby is equally as important as far-reaching ministries. Identify the needs of your town, your neighborhood, and your closest neighbors to determine how God might use you as a significant witness this summer.

For Further Discussion

1. What are the ways your local church is currently ministering to the poor, the sick, and the hurting in your community? Which of these could serve as a springboard for summer ministry?

2. If your church's money, time, and other resources were unlimited, what kinds of creative summer ministries would you do?
3. What is the correct balance in ministry between sharing the gospel and meeting basic human needs?

For Application

1. What are some of the parachurch organizations in your area who are ministering in creative ways? Have someone in the class call them to get ideas on how your church could help them this summer.
2. Invite someone from your church or community, who is making a difference in the lives of others, to speak to the class about their ministry.
3. Invite someone whose life has been changed by a summer ministry to speak to your class about what summer ministry means to them.

Organizations Which Can Help

American Assn. of Christian
 Counselors
P.O. Box 55712
Jackson, MS 39216
(601) 981-1981

Neighborhood Bible Studies
P.O. Box 222
Dobbs Ferry, NY 10522

American Tract Society
1624 N. First Street
Garland, TX 75040

Rock of Our Salvation Evang.
 Free Church
Raleigh Washington, Pastor
118 N Central Avenue
Chicago, IL 60644

Christian Assn. for Psychological
 Studies
P.O. Box 628
Blue Jay, CA 92317
(714) 337-5117

Search Ministries, Inc.
Common Ground Newsletter
P.O. Box 521
Lutherville, MD 21093

Circle Urban Ministries
Glen Kehrein, Director
5806 W Fullerton
Chicago, IL 60639

Urban Family (magazine)
P.O. Box 40125
Pasadena, CA 91104

Int'l. Union of Gospel Missions
1045 Swift N.
North Kansas City, MO 64116

Urban Mission
P.O. Box 27009
Philadelphia, PA 19118

Literacy & Evangelism Int'l.
1800 S. Jackson Avenue
Tulsa, OK 74107

National Center For Fathering
P.O. Box 1918
217 Southwind Place
Manhattan, KS 66502

Willow Creek Association
P.O. Box 3188
Barrington, IL 60011-3188

Worldwide Dental Health
 Service
P.O. Box 7002
Seattle, WA 98133

CREATING AN UNIQUE SUMMER MINISTRY

12

As we have discovered in this book, opportunities for meaningful and creative summer ministries abound. Local churches have a myriad of options from which to choose. But how does a church know if a particular summer ministry is right for them? Should a church try to do as many summer ministries as possible or should a church be selective in its approach? Prayer should be made an important part of your summer ministry planning process. You should pray for wisdom and ask God to give you and your church's leadership team insight as you evaluate the past and plan for the future.

However, prayer alone, while of vital importance, is not enough in itself to create a full-blown summer ministries program. God expects you to exercise the gifts and intelligence He has given His children as you plan your summer ministries program. The following seven-step approach is designed to guide your church through the process of making wise decisions concerning your involvement in summer ministries.

Step One
Evaluate the Summer Ministries You Currently Have

In order to gain insight into where your church should be going in the area of summer ministries, it must be determined where you have been. Evaluation of past summer ministry experiences is an important first step in the process. Keep in mind that you can often learn more from your failures than your successes. Sometimes knowing what not to do is as important as doing what really works well.

Use the following outline to evaluate the summer ministries your church has directed in the past.

1. Name of the Summer Ministry
2. Name of the leader responsible for the ministry

3. How many staff (both paid and volunteer)?
4. What was the budget (both income and expenses)?
5. What were the primary and secondary goals of the ministry?
6. Were these goals accomplished? Why or why not?
7. What are the recommendations of the leadership team (of this summer ministry) concerning next summer?
8. What are the recommendations of the participants of this summer ministry concerning next summer?
9. What are the recommendations of the church leadership regarding the future of this ministry?

Answering these questions will give you a strong indication if any summer ministry should be dropped from the schedule, continued as is next summer, or continued with certain modifications. Although the best time for evaluation is shortly after a ministry has been completed, it is always helpful to check with those who were involved (both leadership and participants) for input, even many months after the completion of the ministry. Be careful not to fall into the trap of feeling you must continue a particular ministry if it is not accomplishing what it was designed to do. At the completion of this section, you should have a good idea of what past programs you want to drop, keep, or modify on your schedule.

Step Two
Survey the Congregation and Community for Input

Although there are biblical instructions telling us what people need (conversion, spiritual growth, a walk of obedience, etc.), we should also provide a means for participants to communicate what they want, like, and dislike. This does not mean a church should only be involved in ministries that meet so-called "felt needs" of people. It does mean we should know the people to whom we desire to minister. For example, last summer your church had a baseball camp for boys 10 to 12 years of age. The camp was successful, so you are planning to do it again this summer. However, suppose you survey your people and find a soccer camp would generate even more interest. Whereas you had only one week of baseball camp last summer, this year it appears you could have three weeks of soccer camp and still not meet the demand. The key is this—you would have never known of this "need" for a soccer camp unless you asked the people you are seeking to serve.

Thus, an important step in your summer ministries planning is to survey your church, and your surrounding community, for their input on what programs you should sponsor this coming summer.

A sample survey form (which can be reproduced) is included in the *Instructor's Guide* for this course. If you want to design your own survey, you should include a demographic section (age, sex, number of kids, year in school, etc.) as well as questions like these:

➡ What summer ministries were you involved in last year? (It will be helpful if you list all of them.)

➡ If the same programs were offered this summer, in which would you or your children participate?

➡ What additional summer ministry programs do you recommend be considered to add to the church's summer ministries schedule this summer?

➡ Would you be willing to volunteer your help in any of the activities in which you have indicated an interest? If so, what skills training do you have?

You should duplicate the survey form and distribute it (with the senior pastor's permission) on a Sunday morning if possible. You should also send surveys to people who were involved (or their children were involved) in one or more of your summer ministries last summer. You may also want to do a random survey of people in your immediate geographical area to find out if they have any interest in your past or future summer ministries programs.

Step Three
Choose the Summer Ministries You Want to Do

As you collect survey forms and tabulate the results, you should carefully compare what the surveys tell you with the evaluation of your leaders and participants from the previous summer. It may be helpful to use the following grid to guide you in making wise decisions regarding the summer ministries program.

Summer Ministry Evaluation	Program #1	Program #2	Program #3	Program #4
Leadership Evaluation				
Participants' Evaluation				
General Church Evaluation				
General Community Evaluation				
Overall Rating				

This "scorecard" will give your church's leadership the data needed to make a wise final decision concerning what programs to adopt for the next summer.

Step Four
Develop a Game Plan for Each Summer Ministry

After ministries are selected for the next summer, the following questions should be answered on each ministry.

Summer Ministry Planning	Program #1	Program #2	Program #3	Program #4
What is the basic outline of the program?				
Target audience?				
Primary/secondary goals?				
Personnel needed?				
Curriculum materials & supplies needed?				
Budget needed?				
Promotion needed?				
When/where?				
Fee or free?				
Follow-up plan?				

Once you have the answers to these questions, you can begin planning for each specific ministry.

Here are some things you should keep in mind as you plan for each ministry.

1. What staff person is responsible for each summer ministry?
2. Are there written ministry descriptions for each position?
3. Are recruitment efforts for the volunteer staff on schedule?
4. Is a training program in place for the volunteer staff?
5. Are promotional efforts planned to communicate to the target audience?
6. Is there sufficient funding in place to cover pre-ministry expenditures?
7. Are all rental sites' reservations confirmed?
8. Are application forms prepared for ministry participants?
9. Are release forms available to be signed by the parents/-guardians of minors?

10. Have you made proper emergency preparations? E.g. First-aid kit, registered nurse on staff, route to closest hospital or other emergency medical facility, etc.?

Answering the above questions is just a beginning point in your planning process. Simply put—planning for a summer ministry is hard work!

Step Five

Create a Summer Ministries Calendar

The leadership team should assign all summer ministries to the master church calendar before publicity is prepared and distributed for each program. Obviously, summer time can mean many possible conflicts in use of church facilities. For summer ministries to be planned effectively, there should be one master church calendar and one person responsible for that calendar. This will not totally eliminate conflicts, but it will help to minimize them.

Once the summer ministry calendar has been agreed upon, it should be mailed to your church's general mailing list, plus the people outside your regular church family who were involved in one of your summer ministries last year. Busy church families will thank you for your thoughtfulness as this calendar will help simplify already busy family life. You should also consider placing poster-size copies of the summer ministries calendar in selected locations inside your church's facilities.

Step Six

Do It!

Finally, all of the advance planning, recruiting, training, promotion and registration is over and you are ready to start your particular summer ministry program. No matter how hard you have worked to this point, there will always be a few details that still have not been covered. At this point, it is good to be reminded of what William Carey (famous missionary to India) is reputed to have said, "Work as if everything depended on you—pray as if everything depended on God." Be sure not to get so caught up in the *process* of ministry that you forget the *purpose* of ministry. Your summer ministry should have the ultimate goal of bringing glory to God as you seek to impact the spiritual lives of your ministry participants. Be sure to "keep your eyes on the prize" and do not be discouraged by minor setbacks or discouragements. If you have done your part faithfully, God is pledged to do His—and He will!

Step Seven

Evaluate Your Summer Ministries

The development of a summer ministry program is a cyclical process. Evaluation is the first step in the process and the last as well. After your summer is over, you should take a critical look at exactly what you have and have not accomplished in your summer ministries program. You should follow the ideas outlined under step one.

You will find that the closer your evaluation is to the end of each program, the more useful it will be. If possible, seek input from all who were involved in each program—participants and workers. Encourage them to be open in their responses. If you have, in the past, demonstrated that you take people's comments seriously, they will usually be willing to share with you how they really feel about the program they are evaluating. By evaluating your summer ministries program promptly at the end of summer, you will have the entire fall and spring months to make provisions for next summer's program of activities.

Summary

There are a multitude of opportunities for dynamic summer ministries. However, for your church to take advantage of those opportunities there must be a commitment to consistent prayer as well as hard work. The place to begin is evaluating the summer ministries your church already conducts. Next, survey the congregation and community for their input as you prepare to choose the ministries you want to do for the upcoming summer. After this decision has been made, you can develop a game plan for each specific ministry. The church will be wise to have a summer ministries calendar to avoid conflicts. By then, it will be time to actually do the ministries you have worked on and prayed for during the past months. After the summer is over, you will want to start the process all over again by evaluating the effectiveness of each ministry.

God has given your church valuable resources which He expects you to invest in ministries which will impact lives for His glory. Is your church prepared to develop a God-honoring Vacation Bible School and other summer ministries which can bring people into a personal relationship with Jesus Christ and assist them in the process of spiritual growth? Children, youth, and adults in your community are waiting for a church which will supply the ministries which will meet their needs. Will your church be the one?

For Further Discussion

1. What is the importance of prayer in the summer ministry planning process? For what should you be praying?
2. Why is evaluation an important step in the planning process?
3. What kinds of summer ministry programs do you think your church and community would respond to positively? Why?
4. List the kinds of things that should be part of emergency preparedness.

5. Why is the development of a master church calendar of special importance?
6. Why is planning for summer ministries called a cyclical process?

For Application

1. What problems could have been avoided in the past in your church's summer ministry program if proper evaluations had been done?
2. Collect as much information as you can (brochures, bulletin announcements, planning schedules, ministry descriptions, budgets, etc.) on the summer ministry programs your church has sponsored in the past. From this material, what can you learn in terms of do's and don'ts that will assist your planning for this summer?
3. Interview two or three people in your church from each major age group (children, teens, adults) regarding their preferences of the summer ministries which your local church should sponsor. Compile your results and present them to the group.
4. Call two or three churches in your local area and find out what type of summer ministries they have done in the past and are planning to do in the future.
5. What summer ministries are of special interest to you? Are you willing to make a commitment of your time this summer to get involved?

Organizations Which Can Help

For more than fifty years the National Association of Evangelicals has existed to bridge local ministry to the larger community of brothers and sisters in Christ. As you discover new avenues for ministry, the many commissions of NAE may become valuable points of contact and shared vision:

National Association Of Evangelicals
P.O. Box 28
Wheaton, IL 60189
FAX 708-665-8575

Commissions:
NAE Evangelism and Home Missions Assoc.
P.O. Box 35000
Colorado Springs, CO 80935
719-599-5999; FAX 719-599-5898

NAE Hispanic Commission
P.O. Box 5747
Cleveland, TN 37320
615-478-7164; FAX 615-478-7888

NAE National Christian Education Association
P.O. Box 535002
Indianapolis, IN 46253-5002
317-244-3660; FAX 317-244-1247

NAE Social Action Commission
309 S. Oak Street
Marysville, OH 43040
513-644-8442

NAE Women's Commission
1445 Boonville Avenue
Springfield, MO 65802
417-862-2781; FAX 417-862-0503

Affiliates:
Evangelical Fellowship of Mission Agencies
1023 15th Street N.W., Ste. 500
Washington, DC 20005
202-789-1011; FAX 202-842-0392

National Association of Christian Child & Family Agencies
3603 N. 7th Avenue
Phoenix, AZ 85013
602-234-1935; FAX 602-234-0022

BIBLIOGRAPHY

Chapter 1

Freese, Doris A. *Vacation Bible School*. Wheaton, IL: Evangelical Training Association, 1977.

More Than Sunday School. Wheaton, IL: Evangelical Training Association, 1992.

Newman, Gene, and Tada, Joni Eareckson. *All God's Children, Ministry with Disabled Persons*. Grand Rapids, MI: Zondervan Publishing, 1993.

Chapter 2

Daniel, Eleanor. *The ABC's of Vacation Bible School*. Cincinnati, OH: Standard Publishing, 1984.

Freese, Doris A. *Vacation Bible School*. Wheaton, IL: Evangelical Training Association, 1977.

Chapter 3

Schneck, Susan, and Strohl, Mary. *Vacation Bible School Ideas and Summertime Fun*. Carthage, IL: Shining Star Publications, 1989.

Wienecke, Jeannette. *Vacation Bible School: A Creative Summer Ministry*. Kansas City: Beacon Hill Press, 1980.

Chapter 4

Fields, Doug. *Help! I'm A Volunteer Youth Worker*. Grand Rapids, MI: Youth Specialties, Zondervan Publishing, 1993.

Leone, Dee. *Vacation Bible School Activities*. Carthage, IL: Shining Star Publications, 1990.

Chapter 5

Cionca, John R. *Solving Church Education's Ten Toughest Problems*. Wheaton, IL: Victor Books, Scripture Press Publications, 1990.

Chapter 6

Barna, George. *Church Marketing*. Ventura, CA: Regal Books, Gospel Light, 1992. Chapter 7.

Fagerstrom, Douglas. *Singles Ministry Handbook, A Practical Guide to Reaching Adult Singles in the Church*. Wheaton, IL: Victor Books, Scripture Press Publications, 1988.

Parrott, Les III. *Helping The Struggling Adolescent, A Guide to Thirty Common Problems for Parents, Counselors, & Youth Workers*. Grand Rapids, MI: Zondervan Publishing, 1993.

Chapter 9

Bertolini, Dewey M. *Back To The Heart Of Youth Work*. Wheaton, IL: Victor Books, 1989.

Bugbee, Bruce L. *Networking, Equipping Those Who Are Seeking To Serve*. Grand Rapids, MI: Zondervan Publishing, 1994.

Fagerstrom, Douglas L. *Singles Ministry Handbook, A Practical Guide to Reaching Adult Singles in the Church*. Wheaton, IL: Victor Books, Scripture Press Publications, 1988.

Gallardo, Marsha. "Short-Term Mission Trips: Developing Hearts for Missions." *Ministries Today, The Magazine About Renewal in Leadership*, July/August 1992. Strang Communications Co., 600 Rinehart Road, Lake Mary, FL 32746.

Keefaver, Larry. *Friends & Faith*. Loveland, CO: Group Books, 1986.

Newton, LaVose. *The Church Library Handbook, Everything You Need To Know To Organize A Church Library Ministry*. Eugene, OR: Harvest House Publishers, 1987.

Shibley, David. "Finding Your Place In World Missions: Eleven Steps For Local Churches." *Ministries Today, The Magazine About Renewal in Leadership*, July/Agust 1992. Strang Communications Co., 600 Rinehart Road, Lake Mary, FL 32746.

Weising, Edward F. & Gwen. *Singleness*. Springfield, MO: Gospel Publishing House, 1982.

Chapter 10

Anthony, Michael J. *Foundations of Ministry: An Introduction to Christian Education for a New Generation*. Wheaton, IL: BridgePoint, Victor Books, Scripture Press, 1992.

Mattson, Lloyd D. *Camping Guideposts*. Chicago: Moody Press, 1972.

_____. *Foul-up or Follow-up?* Wheaton, IL: Victor Books, Scripture Press, 1974.

Wright, H. Norman, and Anthony, Michael J. *Help, I'm a Camp Counselor!* Ventura, CA: Regal Books, 1986.

Chapter 11

McGrath, Alister E. *Intellectuals Don't Need God, Building Bridges To Faith*. Grand Rapids, MI: Zondervan Publishing, 1993.

Smith, Donald K. *Creating Understanding, A Handbook for Communication Across Cultural Landscapes*. Grand Rapids, MI: Zondervan Publishing, 1993.

Strobel, Lee. *Inside The Mind of Unchurched Harry & Mary, How To Reach Friends and Family Who Avoid God and The Church*. Grand Rapids, MI: Zondervan Publishing, 1993.

Washington, Raleigh, and Kehrein, Glen. *Breaking Down Walls*. Chicago, IL: Moody Press, 1993.

Chapter 12

Anderson, Leith. *A Church For The 21st Century, Bringing Change to Your Church to Meet the Challenges of a Changing Society*. Minneapolis, MN: Bethany House Publishers, 1992.

Eaton, Chris, and Hurst, Kim. *Vacations With A Purpose*. Colorado Springs, CO: NavPress, 1991.

Kadlecek, Jo. "Special Report #12." *Current Thoughts & Trends Supplement*, July 1993. The Navigators, 7899 Lexington Drive, Colorado Springs, CO 80920.

McGrath, Alister E. *Intellectuals Don't Need God, & Other Modern Myths*. Grand Rapids, MI: Zondervan Publishing, Academic and Professional Books, 1993.

Self, Margaret M., ed. *Effective Year-round Bible Ministries*. Ventura, CA: Regal Books, 1980.